Contents

THE COUNTRYSIDE AND THE LAW

THE COUNTRYSIDE

AND

THE LAW

by

Charles Fox

DAVID & CHARLES : NEWTON ABBOT

ISBN 0 7153 5353 5

Set in 11/12 point Times Roman
and printed in Great Britain by
Bristol Typesetting Company Limited
for David & Charles (Publishers) Limited
South Devon House Newton Abbot Devon

Preface

This book is a guide to the law about the countryside as it affects both the people who live in the country and visitors from the cities and towns. I have described the main principles, and wherever possible I have illustrated them from decisions in the courts. It is in the cases that the law really comes to life. Readers who need more detail should turn to the notes which are arranged chapter by chapter at the end of the book. The notes refer them to the sources, the Acts of Parliament, the official Law Reports, and, much more rarely, statutory instruments.

The book is primarily about the law in England and Wales. Scotland and Northern Ireland have separate systems of law. Basically their systems are not very different from the systems in England and Wales, but they do both have certain special features. The important differences are mentioned briefly in paragraphs at the end of each chapter.

I have assumed that the present Animals Bill will become law, and refer to it as the Animals Act 1971

March 1971

Introduction

The changes in the countryside which have occurred during the last two centuries can hardly be exaggerated. Two hundred years ago, most British people still lived and worked on the land. Cities and towns were small, so that almost everybody, even in London, lived within easy riding or walking distance of open country.

The industrial revolution and the growth of the population have made great inroads on the countryside. Every year, more land is needed for houses, shops, and factories. New towns are built and old towns become larger.

At the same time, there is greater pressure on the countryside which remains. Many townspeople long for the amenities which the country possesses, for the opportunity of sport or exercise in a pleasant environment, for peace and quiet, and for the enjoyment of beautiful landscapes. That desire generates a demand for more housing in rural areas, for better roads, and for facilities like camping sites and caravan parks, which may destroy the very beauties which people come to see.

Townspeople must have the opportunity to enjoy the peace and beauty of the countryside, but they must not be allowed to spoil the countryside. These are the two main ideas behind one of the most important of the recent Acts of Parliament which affects the country, the Countryside Act 1968.

1 The Countryside Commission

The National Parks Commission came in existence in 1949, many years after national parks had been established in the United States of America and in some other countries. The commission was given the duty of designating suitable districts as national parks or as areas of outstanding natural beauty and of advising as to their future. In 1968, under the Countryside Act, the commission was also given certain duties to perform in relation to the countryside as a whole, and it was renamed the Countryside Commission.

the commission

The members of the commission are appointed by the Secretary of State for the Environment, and the Secretary of State for Wales. Salaries may be paid, but members who receive them are disqualified from election to the House of Commons. In Wales and Monmouthshire, certain powers are exercised by a special committee known as the Committee for Wales. The commission must report to the secretaries of state every year. Reports are laid before both Houses of Parliament.[1]

the countryside duties

The commission has a general duty to keep a watchful eye on all matters which affect the countryside of England and Wales. In particular, it must see that the countryside is not spoiled and that members of the public have greater means of access and better facilities for enjoyment. The commission must always keep in mind the needs of agriculture and forestry, and the economic and social interests of rural areas. It must, with other bodies, take steps to protect lakes, rivers, and the coast against pollution.[2]

establishing national parks

Though the commission has been given this new general duty to perform, the national parks and the 'areas of outstanding natural beauty' remain its chief concern. The commission from time to time selects areas of land in England and Wales which, because of their beauty and their value for open-air recreation, require special preservation. The more important of these areas become national parks.

When the commission selects an area in which it proposes to establish a national park, it must start consultations with the local authorities which are likely to be affected. If there is no substantial opposition the commission makes an order designating the area as a national park. Due notice of the order must be given to the public, and there must be an opportunity for objections. The Secretary of State for the Environment, or the Secretary of State of Wales, may then confirm the order.

At the time of writing, ten national parks have been established: the Peak District National Park, the Lake District National Park, the Snowdonia National Park, the Dartmoor National Park, the Pembrokeshire Coast National Park, the North York Moors National Park, the Yorkshire Dales National Park, the Exmoor National Park, the Northumberland National Park, and the Brecon Beacons National Park. The establishment of an eleventh national park, in Mid Wales, is under active consideration.[3]

designating areas of outstanding natural beauty

The areas of outstanding natural beauty are selected for similar reasons. The areas are, however, normally smaller than the national parks, and not so important. The procedure for consultation and objection is similar to (but not precisely the same as) that in the case of national parks. Orders are confirmed by one of the secretaries of state.

At the time of writing, the commission has designated twenty-eight areas of outstanding natural beauty: Anglesey, Cannock Chase, Chichester Harbour, the Chilterns, Cornwall, the Cotswolds, Dedham Vale, East Devon, North Devon, South Devon, Dorset, the Forest of Bowland, Gower, East Hampshire, the South Hampshire Coast, the Kent Downs, Lleyn, the Malvern Hills, the Norforlk Coast, the Northumberland Coast, the Quantock Hills, the Shropshire Hills, the Solway Coast, the Suffolk Coast and Heaths, the Surrey Hills, the Sussex Downs, the Isle of Wight and the Wye Valley.[4]

giving advice

The commission is instructed to provide a comprehensive advisory service. It may be called upon by the Government, by local authorities, by public bodies, and in some cases even by ordinary citizens, to give advice about any matter affecting the countryside. It may charge for its services. It cannot, however, do more than advise; it cannot compel.

At present, the commission is asked to advise mainly about the national parks and the areas of outstanding natural beauty. After designation, the commission carries out studies and decides what action ought to be taken to preserve natural beauty and to provide facilities for the public. The commission then makes recommendations to the Secretary of State for the Environment or to the Secretary of State for Wales and to the local planning authorities. From time to time the commission asks for progress reports from the local planning authorities and reviews the work which has been carried out.

Not later than three months after an order designating a national park has been made, every local planning authority in the area must consult with the commission as to how the park is to be administered. If the park is wholly within one planning area, a special planning committee for the park is generally appointed. But when two or more planning areas are involved, it is usual for a joint planning board to be established. In either event the Secretary of State for the

13

Environment, or the Secretary of State for Wales, has a right to nominate some members, and the commission suggests people for nomination. The committee or board exercises the functions of the local planning authority within the park.

When the administrative arrangements have been completed, the commission assists the new authorities in making plans for providing accommodation, access for open-air recreation, and other facilities for visitors. It suggests what bylaws the park ought to have, and what access agreements with local landowners should be made. It looks keenly at proposals for development within the park and tells the planning authorities when it thinks that a particular proposal is detrimental to the park.

In the case of the areas of outstanding natural beauty, there are no special administrative arrangements to be made. The commission, however, advises the local authorities on bylaws, access agreements, and proposals for development.

The commission advises the Secretaries of State on applications by local authorities for exchequer grants for countryside purposes.[5]

affording assistance

In some cases conservation and the provision of amenities for the public may present special problems and require the help of experts. The commission has a duty to warn the administrative authorities of possible difficulties. If the authorities then ask for help, the commission may provide the services of its own employees or of outside experts, and make an appropriate charge.[6]

providing information

The commission must provide an information service about the countryside and about places of particular interest in rural areas. It must try to encourage a proper standard of behaviour on the part of visitors, and it must prepare and publish a countryside code.

The national parks and the areas of outstanding natural beauty, and the long-distance footpaths, like the Pennine Way, must be covered in detail. Guidebooks and leaflets must deal with such subjects as history, natural features, plants and animals, and places of architectural merit.[7]

experimental projects

Finally, the commission may carry out special projects relating to conservation or to the provision of amenities for the public. The idea is to illustrate new methods for the benefit, especially, of the administrative authorities. The commission may acquire land for this purpose.

The commission may also help to finance the carrying out of special projects by private persons or organisations. It may make grants or loans with ministerial or treasury approval. Grants may not be more than three-quarters of the cost of a project, and conditions may be imposed. The National Trust, though strictly speaking it is not a private body, may receive grants.[8]

Scotland

A separate Countryside Commission for Scotland was established under the Countryside (Scotland) Act 1967. Its members are appointed by the Secretary of State for Scotland, and its powers and responsibilities are similar to those of the Countryside Commission for England and Wales.

No national parks have yet been designated. There are, however, three national forest parks, Glen More in the Cairngorms, Queen Elizabeth Park in Argyllshire and Glen Trool in south-west Scotland. Wester Ross, Glen Affric, the Cairngorms, Glen Coe, and the Trossachs have been designated as areas of outstanding natural beauty.

The National Trust for Scotland may receive grants for countryside purposes.[9]

Northern Ireland

The important Act in Northern Ireland is the Amenity Lands Act (Northern Ireland) 1965. The Act gives the Minister of Development powers to acquire areas of land in order to preserve their natural beauty and amenity or to establish nature reserves. Access roads and paths may be built and facilities like toilets and restaurants may be provided where necessary.

The Ministry may designate a national park or an area of outstanding natural beauty by order. There are provisions for the hearing of objections to draft orders. The Ulster Countryside Committee gives advice, but its powers and responsibilities are not so great as those of the Countryside Commission in England and Wales. There is also a Nature Reserves Committee to advise about reserves and other areas of scientific interest.

Notes to this chapter are on page 183.

16

2 Government and Local Authorities

Until 1909, with few exceptions, a landowner could do what he liked with his land, so long as he did not infringe the rights of other landowners. He could put up buildings which were unsuitable in themselves or which were entirely out of keeping with their surroundings. A large part of the countryside was ruined by unrestricted speculative development.

The first Act which was concerned with town planning was the Housing, Town Planning, etc Act, 1909. This Act, and a number of other Acts which followed it, were concerned only with towns. It was not until the Town and Country Planning Act 1932 came into operation that planning was extended to the countryside.

Under the Town and Country Planning Act 1932, every local authority was empowered to prepare a scheme showing what development would be permitted in the area of that authority. If land was developed in a manner which was not permitted by the scheme, the authority could compel the owner to pull down buildings and generally to do whatever was necessary to restore the land to its former condition.

The weakness of the Town and Country Planning Act 1932 was that the preparation of schemes was optional. Many local authorities did not bother. Even if an authority did decide to prepare a scheme there would nearly always be a long delay between the decision and the final approval of the scheme. During that period much building might take place.

The only kind of development which was restricted in the country as a whole was development along main roads. After the first world war, many arterial roads were made. Builders acquired thin strips of land on both sides of these roads, and put up houses. They could sell these houses more cheaply than houses on a building estate because they did not have to bear the cost of making up roads.

In many places the landscape was completely spoiled by ribbon development. The main objections at the time, however, were that living in the new houses were dangerous, and that the roads were becoming choked with local traffic. Parliament tackled the problem by passing the Restriction of Ribbon Development Act 1935. The act, which was applied to major roads and some minor roads, prohibited the erection of buildings near certain roads without the consent of the highway authority.

General planning control was only extended to the whole country when the Town and Country Planning (Interim Development) Act 1943 was passed.[1] Since that time, several town and country planning acts have been passed and they have gradually strengthened the system of planning control.

They have not, of course, prevented more land from being used for housing as the population has expanded. The countryside continues to diminish and urban and suburban areas continue to increase. Much development is still badly conceived, but at least it is not entirely indiscriminate and unplanned. Some effort is being made to ensure that the whole of the countryside is not spoiled, though oddly enough the Crown is still exempt from planning control.

responsibility for planning

The responsibility for town and country planning is divided. The Secretary of State for the Environment and the Secretary of State for Wales between them frame a national policy for the use and development of land throughout England and Wales.[2] They ensure, so far as they can, that the national policy is applied consistently everywhere.

The local planning authorities, that is to say the county councils and the county borough councils, and in some cases a joint board, execute the national policy in their own areas. Certain powers may be delegated to rural district and urban district councils.

development plans

Under the Town and Country Planning Act 1968, every local planning authority which has not already done so must make a geographical survey of its own area, with a view to deciding the form and extent of future development.[3] The survey must cover all matters affecting the planning of the area such as the economy, the communications, and the size and distribution of the population. When the survey has been completed, the authority must publish the results in such a way as to bring them to the attention of everyone who is likely to be interested. The authority must consider any representations which may be made.

The authority then prepares a general development plan. The plan is called a structure plan, because it gives a picture of development and intended development in the area as a whole. The plan shows in a broad way what land is likely to be built upon, and what land will remain open country as long as the authority can foresee. When the plan has been drawn up, copies must be made available for public inspection at the council offices. The public then has an opportunity for a limited period to make objections in England to the Secretary of State for the Environment, or in Wales to the Secretary of State for Wales. After this time, the Secretary of State concerned may approve or reject the plan. Plans must be reviewed at least once in every five years.

A local planning authority may also, when it appears desirable, prepare a local plan for any part of its area. Local plans for districts in which a substantial amount of development or re-development is intended to take place, must be prepared. The idea is to show the detailed effect of the general proposals in the area concerned. Objections may be made after a local plan is published. There are provisions for holding local inquiries about local plans, and the Secretary of State concerned may intervene in certain circumstances.[4]

general development orders

Development plans merely show where development is

likely to be permitted, and where it is not likely to be permitted. They do not give permission for development. In the normal way, no building operations can be started until a specific application to the local planning authority has been made and the application has been granted.

The Secretary of State for the Environment and his predecessors, however, have made a number of general development orders which permit the carrying out of certain minor developments. In the cases covered by the orders, there is no need to apply for permission to the local planning authority. One general development order, for example, covers small improvements to private houses; it is important to read the order carefully to discover exactly what is, and what is not, allowed. Another general development order permits the putting up of fences and walls, with specified limits as to height. A third general development order authorises the erection of certain temporary buildings. There are many other orders.

Two of these particularly affect the countryside. They allow the erection of buildings for agriculture and forestry. There are conditions as to size, height, and proximity to roads. Where agricultural buildings are concerned, the ground area must not exceed 5,000 square feet, two or more buildings in the same unit sometimes having to be treated as one for this purpose. The height must not exceed 40 feet, or 10 feet if the building is within two miles of the perimeter of an airfield. Buildings must not be erected within 80 feet of classified roads. In certain specified landscape areas, however, mainly in Wales, Derbyshire, and the Lake District, buildings must not be erected until notice has been given to the local planning authority, which may impose conditions as to design and external appearance.[5]

planning applications

When a proposed development is not covered by a general development order, a specific application to the local planning authority must be made. In some cases the applications have to be advertised, and sometimes warning notices have to be given, for example, by a landlord to an agricultural tenant who will be affected. Planning authorities must keep registers of applications for planning permission, and the registers must be open to public inspection.

When considering applications, planning authorities take into account development plans, and any other factors such as general national policy. The Secretary of State for the Environment and his predecessors have issued a large number of circulars to help authorities in dealing with planning applications. One circular, for example, covers new houses in the country. In another circular the need to safeguard agricultural land is emphasised. There is also a book about buildings and the countryside.[6]

planning decisions

A planning authority may decide an application in one of three ways. It may grant permission for the proposed development unconditionally. It may grant permission subject to such conditions as it thinks fit. It may entirely refuse permission, in many cases without compensation. Sometimes applications for planning permission are made in outline, and outline permission may be given. This means that details of the proposed building have to be settled between the applicant and the planning authority later on. The substantive application should be made within three years.[7]

planning appeals

If planning permission is refused, or is made conditional, the applicant may appeal in England to the Secretary of State for the Environment, or in Wales and Monmouthshire to the Secretary of State for Wales.[8] The Secretaries of State normally delegate their powers of deciding appeals to specially appointed officers. In cases of unusual difficulty, or where matters of national or regional importance are raised, however, a planning inquiry commission consisting of a chairman and between two and four other members may hold a local inquiry. The commission reports to the Secretary of State, who then decides the appeal himself. In all cases, the applicant and the planning authority have a further right of appeal on questions of law to the High Court.[9]

Fawcett Properties Ltd v Buckingham County Council[10] was a very important planning appeal which concerned agricultural cottages. In 1952, a farmer at Chalfont St Giles in Buckinghamshire, which was in the metropolitan green belt, applied to the county council for planning permission to build two cottages at the farm. He said that the farm was rather isolated, and it was necessary, in order to get farm workers, to offer them living accommodation.

The council granted planning permission subject to a condition that 'the occupation of the houses shall be limited to persons whose employment . . . is . . . in agriculture or in an industry mainly dependent upon agriculture.' The council said that the land was shown as green-belt land on its development plan, and it was not therefore prepared to permit the building of houses which were not connected with the use of the adjoining land for agriculture.

In 1956 the cottages were acquired by Fawcett Properties Ltd. The company contended that the restriction was unreasonable, and asked the council to remove it. The council refused. The company appealed, and eventually its appeal reached the House of Lords. The judges decided that the attitude of the county council was justified. They pointed out that if the restriction were removed, the property company could sell or let the cottages to town workers. 'That part of Buckinghamshire would see a piece of sporadic and isolated development which was the very thing that the county plan condemned.'

'The effect of the condition' Lord Denning said 'is to ensure that the cottages will be occupied by persons who will help to maintain the normal life and character of this part of the green belt and not by outsiders to use as a dormitory. The cottages are for farm workers or for men who work at the smithy shoeing horses or at the mill grinding the corn or at the sawmill cutting up wood, or in modern parlance at a milk depot bottling the milk or at the repair shop mending the tractors and so forth. They are not for people who go up and down to London every day.'

enforcement orders and stop orders

A local planning authority has wide powers to stop unauthorised development, but in cases in which the unauthorised development consists of building, mining, or engineering operations, it must act within four years of the time when the unauthorised development began. The enforcement procedure usually begins with a visit by a surveyor employed by the authority, who can enter property without permission. If the surveyor reports that unauthorised development has taken place, the authority will, if the matter appears to be at all serious, serve an 'enforcement notice' on the occupier of the property, and also the owner if he is a different person. The notice states that development has taken place without permission, or that a condition of planning permission has not been observed, and gives details. The owner and occupier are required to restore the land to its former condition within a time limit. They may be compelled to alter, or even to demolish, a building. The notice does not, however, take effect for at least twenty-eight days.

In cases in which unauthorised development is actually going on at the time when the enforcement notice is served, the authority may also serve a 'stop notice'. Development must then cease, normally within three days. Disobedience to a stop notice may lead to prosecution and a heavy fine.

During the period of grace before the enforcement order takes effect, there is a right of appeal on a number of grounds to the Secretary of State for the Environment or the Secretary of State for Wales,[11] and from them on a point of law to the High Court. Appeals are normally heard by a specially appointed officer. The appellant may contend, for example, that planning permission was not necessary because the development was covered by a general order. If the officer, or the court, decides that the appellant is correct, the enforcement order will be quashed, and the appellant will be entitled to compensation for any loss he may have suffered because of a stop notice. Alternatively, he may contend that though he omitted to ask for permission to develop, the building does not conflict with the development plan and ought to be allowed. If he succeeds in this contention, the enforcement notice will be quashed but he will not get compensation.

An enforcement notice takes effect either at the end of the period of grace or after an appeal has proved unsuccessful. The required work must then be done within the time limit specified in the notice. If the owner defaults, he may be prosecuted. The planning authority may itself do the work and recover the expense from him.[12]

discontinuance orders

The enforcement order and the stop order may be used negatively to prevent the environment from deteriorating, or deteriorating further. The discontinuance order may be used positively, in order to improve the environment.

In the interests of the proper planning, including the amenity, of an area, the local planning authority may serve a discontinuance order on the owner or occupier of any property. The order may require the pulling down of a building or the discontinuance of the use of land for particular purpose. The owner of a dog kennels may, for example, be forced to move elsewhere. Alternatively an order may say that a use is to be discontinued unless certain conditions are observed, for example, that the amount of noise is reduced. There is no four-year time limit: the building may have been standing or the use may have been going on for many years. Orders do not, however, take effect unless they are confirmed by the Secretary of State for the Environment or the Secretary of State for Wales[13] and owners and occupiers have a right of appeal.

Discontinuance orders, like enforcement and stop orders, may be enforced by prosecution, and the planning authority may do the required work itself. When a person suffers loss as a result of a discontinuance order, however, he is entitled to compensation and he may even be able to compel the authority to buy the land from him.[14]

caravan sites

Holidays in caravans are becoming very popular. Especially near the coast and in the national parks, there is a strong demand for seasonal caravan sites. There are also a large number of permanent caravan sites. In many places, caravans can seriously disfigure a landscape and there are, therefore, strict controls.

If a farmer, or any other person, wishes to use part of his land as a caravan site, he must first of all obtain planning permission.[15] This by itself, however, is generally not enough. Normally he must also obtain a site licence from the local authority. Local authorities must keep registers of licences.[16]

The local authority cannot normally refuse to grant a site licence, but may impose conditions. The Secretary of State for the Environment and his predecessors have drafted model conditions as to the layout of caravan sites. Local authorities must have regard to these conditions, but they need not impose them rigidly.

Conditions may require that trees or bushes are planted in order to screen the site. They may restrict the use of the site to certain months in the year and may restrict the number of caravans which may be stationed on the site at any one time. They may require that no caravan is to be stationed there unless it conforms to specification as to size and is in good repair. They may specify in detail where the caravans are to be put, and they may prohibit the parking of cars and the putting up of tents. They may require that the owner of the site provides proper sanitary arrangements for people living in the caravans. Local authorities may alter conditions at any time, though holders of site licences have rights to make representations and to appeal to the courts. Licences must be displayed prominently on sites for more than three caravans.[17]

If the owner of a site thinks that a condition which has been attached to his licence is unfair, he may appeal against it to the magistrates' court for the area. If the court is satisfied that a condition is unduly burdensome, the court may vary or annul the condition. There is a further right of appeal, on questions of law, to the High Court.[18]

In the case of *Esdell Caravan Parks Ltd v Hemel Hempstead Rural District Council*,[19] the owners of a site contended that a condition limiting the number of caravans to be stationed on the site was unreasonable. The company owned a five-acre field, known as the Stagg Farm Caravan Site, at Hogspit Bottom, Bovingdon, in Hertfordshire. Twenty-four caravans had been stationed there for many years before the passing of the Caravan Sites and Control of Development Act 1960. The Hemel Hempstead Rural District Council granted a site licence under the Act to the company. One of the conditions in the licence was there should never be more than twenty-four caravans on the site.

The company appealed against the condition to the Berkhamsted magistrates' court. It said that under the model standards of the ministry, the maximum number of caravans permissible would be eighty. It wanted the court to vary the condition so as to permit it to lay out the field 'as a site for seventy-eight good-class caravans connected to all main services.' There were no public health reasons, it said, why seventy-eight caravans should not be allowed, and the value of the field would be increased fourfold.

The Hemel Hempstead Rural District Council replied that Hogspit Bottom was a tiny hamlet in the London green belt. If the number of caravans were increased a variety of problems would arise. Above all, it would be against the general planning policy for the area. There were severe restrictions on building new houses, and all recent applications for planning permission had been refused. The local schools were overcrowded, public transport was poor, and the nearest places for shopping were two miles away. There would be more cars entering and leaving the field, and the narrow lanes in the area would become more hazardous for traffic. This would cause some damage to the amenities of the area and some additional noise for the people who lived at Hogspit Bottom. Furthermore the view from some gardens would be spoiled.

The court accepted the arguments of the council, and refused to alter the condition. The company appealed to the High Court. The Court of Appeal said that the magistrates were right. The number of caravans could not be increased.

The officers of local authorities have a right, after giving twenty-four hours' notice, to enter caravan sites in order to satisfy themselves that conditions are being observed. If on any site they find that conditions are not being oberved, the local authority may prosecute the owner of the site. On the third conviction, the licence may be revoked.[20]

There are a number of important exceptions to the general rule that a site licence must be obtained before caravans can be stationed on any land. No site licence is necessary for the placing of a caravan or caravans in the grounds of a private house if the use is 'incidental to the enjoyment' of the house. Suppose, for example, a farmer employs a married son on the farm. The son and his family sleep in a caravan in the farmyard or in the orchard, but they also use the kitchen and the living room of the farm house. The use of the caravan by the son and his family would almost certainly be 'incidental to the enjoyment' of the farm house.

A landowner may, without having a site licence, allow his land to be used occasionally by people travelling with caravans. Occasional use means use for not more than twenty-eight days in any year. The owner must not allow more than three caravans at a time to be on the land. When the land is less than five acres in extent, only one caravan is normally permitted. No caravan may remain on the land for longer than two nights.

A farmer may, without licence, provide a caravan site for seasonal workers. This exception would cover, for example, the stationing of caravans on farm land by hop pickers during the season.[21]

As caravans can spoil the appearance of common land, rural district councils have been given powers by order to restrict or completely prohibit the stationing of caravans on commons and village greens. When an order is made, a copy must be posted on the land. People with caravans who disobey orders may be prosecuted.[22]

In some places, there are not enough privately owned caravan sites to meet the demand. Local authorities have the power to buy land, compulsorily if necessary, to establish new sites for the use of holidaymakers and for those who intend to live in their caravans permanently. Authorities may

27

manage the sites themselves or they may let them to other persons.[23]

gypsies

County councils have a duty to provide adequate caravan sites for gypsies 'residing in or resorting to' their counties. County councils decide what sites are required, and then confer with the district councils concerned. In the event of disagreement about a proposal, the district council may appeal to the Secretary of State for the Environment or the Secretary of State for Wales.[24] County councils acquire the necessary land for sites, but district councils administer the sites once they have been established.

When the Secretary of State is satisfied that there are sufficient sites for gypsies 'residing in or resorting to' a county, he may on the application of the county council designate the county as a prohibited area. A gypsy who in a prohibited area lives in a caravan by the side of the road, or unoccupied land, or on occupied land without the consent of the occupier, commits a criminal offence for which he may be prosecuted. In prohibited areas, local authorities may apply to magistrates' courts for removal orders, authorising them to remove unlawful encampments. Any person who obstructs the carrying out of a removal order commits a criminal offence for which he may be prosecuted.[25]

open land

All too often, waste land becomes a rubbish dump. Local planning authorities have power to compel the owners and occupiers of gardens, empty sites, and other open land, to keep their property tidy. When an authority believes that the amenity of any part of its area or for any adjoining area is 'seriously injured' by the condition in which a piece of open land is being kept, the authority may serve a notice on the owner or occupier. The notice requires the owner or occupier to take specific steps to stop the nuisance within a certain period.

If the owner or occupier believes that the notice was wrongly served, he may appeal against it to the local magistrates' court, and from there to quarter sessions (when the Courts Act 1971 comes into operation, the Crown Court) and the High Court. The owner or occupier may take issue with the planning authority on several points. He may contend that the condition of the land does not seriously injure the amenities of the area or that the land is not open land. He may argue that the requirements of the notice are excessive, or that the period of notice is too short.

A successful appeal on the ground that land does not fall within the legal definition of 'garden, vacant site, or other open land' may defeat the efforts of the local planning authority to remove a serious eyesore. The case of *Stephens v Cuckfield Rural District Council*[26] concerned a plot of land in Tilgate Forest in Sussex. In 1939, Stephens erected timber and metal buildings with iron roofs on the land. For many years he used the land and the buildings as a sawmill for sawing trees cut in the forest. In 1955, however, he closed the sawmill and let the land to a company which carried on a car-breaking business. At about the same time, he enclosed the land with a wire fence and concrete posts. The activities of the car-breaking company turned the land almost into a scrapyard, and in 1957 the Cuckfield Rural District Council served a notice on Stephens. The Council claimed that the condition of the plot, which it described as 'open land', was causing serious injury to the amenity of the forest, and ordered Stephens to 'remove all cars, car bodies, and machinery'. Stephens appealed against the notice. He contended that the land was not a 'garden, vacant site, or other open land'.

The Court of Appeal decided that he was right. Lord Justice Upjohn said that whether land satisfies the description of 'open land' must be treated as a question to be answered by a consideration of all the relevant circumstances of the case. 'In this case, the plot of land in respect of which the notice has been served is open to the air and unbuilt upon, but it is fenced and used for the purpose of a business of a car-breakers' yard, some part of which business is carried on within a building which this piece of land surrounds. None of these circumstances is in itself decisive of the matter but each points to the conclusion which we reach without much difficulty on looking at the matter as a whole that this plot cannot properly be described as open land . . .'

The Cuckfield Rural District Council lost its appeal and the land, presumably, continued to be an eyesore. This decision does not, however, mean that the carrying-on of a business is always a sufficient excuse. Each case is decided on its own facts.

In the case of *Britt v Buckinghamshire County Council*[27] the notice was upheld. The case involved some land at Prestwood in the Chilterns. Britt, who was a motor-vehicle scrap dealer, had bought the plot, which was then being worked as a smallholding, in 1946. He continued to farm part of the land, but began to use the rest as a dump for the lorries and spare parts of lorries in which he dealt. As the years went by, the vehicle and spare-part dealing increased and the agricultural work diminished. Eventually the land was covered with lorries and spare parts of all kinds. The matter was reported to the county council, and it served a notice on Britt complaining that the amenity of part of its area was seriously injured by the condition of his land. In the schedule to the notice, the land was described as 'unsightly, disorderly, and seriously injurious to amenity' in that it was permanently covered with old motor vehicles and parts. The notice ordered Britt to clear out the lorries and the scrap and to put the land into a tidy condition.

Britt appealed against the notice, and the appeal went up to the Court of Appeal. Counsel for Britt argued that open-land notices were designed to deal with injury to amenity when it arose from the condition rather than the use of land. They were intended to cover cases where there was no effective use of land but its condition was injurious to amenity through untidiness or decay, inactivity or neglect. In the present case, if the notice were upheld, Britt would lose his whole livelihood and receive not a penny in compensation.

The court rejected the argument. 'There is no question,' said Lord Justice Sellers, 'that the whole of this area is rightly described as an eyesore. It infringes the provisions [of the town and country planning law] in that it seriously injures the amenities of that locality. In these circumstances, the order was rightly made.' Lord Justice Harman added 'It is said that the man who is told to abate an eyesore ought to be compensated for it. That seems to me to be a most astonishing doctrine . . . I can see no reason why this man, who has for years made the country hideous by his goings on, should not be made to put his house in order, and no reason at all why he should be paid by the public for doing it . . . This appeal fails.'

If the owner or occupier of land does not take the steps required by a notice in the time allowed and 'does anything which has the effect of continuing or aggravating the injury caused by the condition of the land' he may be prosecuted. In all cases where the requirements of a notice are not met, the planning authority may do the necessary work itself and recover the cost.[28]

dumping refuse

Local authorities are bound to provide dumps for the free use of people living in their areas. If a local authority considers that rubbish which has been dumped on land without lawful authority is detrimental to the amenities of the neighbourhood, it may, after giving notice to the owner or occupier of the land in question, remove the rubbish. Local authorities must remove abandoned motor vehicles. The deliberate dumping of large objects like motor vehicles and parts of motor vehicles 'on any land in the open air or on any other land forming part of a highway,' is an offence.[29]

The dropping of litter 'in, into or from any place in the open air to which the public are entitled or permitted to have access without payment' is also an offence. Rather oddly, the leaving of litter in places where an admission fee is charged, like a country house, is not covered. It is immaterial that the money goes to charity; and so, for example, gardens open under the National Gardens Scheme or on Gardeners' Sundays, are not covered. Local councils, the police, and private persons can bring proceedings.[30]

advertisements

The Secretary of State for the Environment and his predecessors have made regulations to restrict the display of advertisements. Local planning authorities may require the removal of advertisements which contravene the regulations. Persons displaying such advertisements may be prosecuted.[31]

The present regulations apply to all advertisements with minor exceptions. One of the exceptions relating to advertisements displayed on enclosed land is of some interest in the country. To qualify, the advertisements must not be readily visible from outside, from parts of the land to which there is a public right of access, or from public rights of way through the land. Enclosed land means 'land which is wholly or for the most part enclosed within a hedge, fence or wall'.

The consent of the Secretary of State for the Environment, the Secretary of State for Wales,[32] or the local planning authority is required for the display of all other advertisements. In some cases, however, consent is deemed to be granted. These include advertisements which were already being displayed in 1948, public notices such as announcements about elections, and small nameplates for houses and other buildings. Consent is also deemed to be granted for the display of advertisements of a temporary nature, such as 'for sale' notices on houses, and notices of forthcoming cattle sales, and of local events generally, though there are stringent requirements as to size. The Secretary of State may, however, by order in specific areas, require that express consent is obtained before even advertisements of any of these kinds are displayed. Moreover planning authorities may in many cases serve discontinuance orders on advertisers and the owners of land requiring particular notices to be removed. There is a right of appeal against discontinuance notices to the Secretary of State.

Unless an advertisement is of one of the exempt categories, or consent is deemed to be granted, an application for express consent must be made. Applications may be refused where the interests of amenity or public safety demand. Questions of amenity arise in places where there is 'any feature of historic, architectural, cultural, or similar interest.'

Local planning authorities have the power, after consultation with rural district councils, to make orders designating areas of special control. Rural areas and areas 'which . . . require special protection on the grounds of amenity' may be designated in this way. Orders must be approved by the Secretary of State for the Environment or the Secretary of State for Wales.[33] There are opportunties for members of the public to make objections before approval is given. Certain advertisements only may, by permission, be displayed in areas of special control. The advertisements which may be allowed include public notices, notices of forthcoming events, time-tables, and 'for sale' notices. They also include advertisements on business premises, for example garage forecourts, and advertisements relating to travelling circuses and fairs. Advertisements must not exceed specified sizes. Where they think fit planning authorities may order the discontinuance of the display of advertisements.

All advertisements, whether or not they are in areas of special control, must be kept neat and tidy.[34]

tree preservation orders

Trees play an important part in the landscape of both town and country and local planning authorities may make tree-preservation orders in the interests of amenity. If they grant planning permission for development they must ensure that there will be an adequate number of trees when the development is complete, and they may also make tree-preservation orders in the exercise of this duty.

Orders prohibit the cutting down, topping or lopping, or the deliberate destruction of trees, groups of trees (apart from dying or dead trees), or woodland, without the consent of the authority. Where consent is given, the consent may be made subject to conditions. Orders may also provide for the re-planting of woodlands which are felled in the course of forestry operations.

Planning authorities must ensure that copies of tree-preservation orders are available for inspection in the district to which they relate, and must send copies of orders to the owners

C   33

and occupiers of land affected by them. When orders are made, objectors have a right to make representations to the Secretary of State for the Environment or the Secretary of State for Wales.[35] Orders have to be confirmed by the Secretary of State before they come into operation.

Any person who contravenes a tree-preservation order is liable to be prosecuted; on conviction he may be fined up to £250 or twice the value of the tree. The High Court may make an injunction to stop further disobedience. Where trees are removed or destroyed, the owner of the land has a duty to plant trees of an appropriate size and species to replace them, and if he does not do so, the planning authority may serve an enforcement notice on him. The owner however has a right of appeal against the enforcement notice to the Secretary of State. Under an enforcement notice, if the owner defaults, the planning authority may do all necessary work and recover the cost from him.[36]

In the case of Attorney General v Melville Construction Co Ltd[37] the company was carrying out development on land at Bolton in Lancashire, which was the subject of a tree-preservation order. It had cut down two trees and seriously damaged twenty-three others. The Bolton Corporation referred the matter to the Attorney General who applied for an injunction in the High Court. The injunction was granted. Mr. Justice Megarry said that the property company was causing irremediable damage: 'A tree which has once been destroyed remains destroyed and cannot be replaced.'

historic buildings

Many landscapes would be marred if buildings were altered or removed. In one place, a street of thatched cottages, in another place a country house, in another a ruined castle on a hill, has a vital part to play in the landscape.

The Secretary of State for the Environment and the Secretary of State for Wales have a duty to compile lists of buildings of special architectural or historic interest.[38] A building may qualify if, though not in itself of particular interest, its exterior contributes to the architectural or historic interest of any group of buildings of which it forms part. Listed buildings receive special protection. When considering an application for permission to alter or to reconstruct a listed building, the planning authority must pay 'special regard to the desirability of preserving the building or any features of special architectural or historic interest which it possesses'. If permission is granted, conditions that particular features are preserved or that original materials are used in the reconstruction, may be imposed.

Any person who without authority demolishes or alters or extends a listed building 'in any manner which would affect its character as a building of special architectural or historic interest', or who fails to comply with a condition attached to a consent, is liable to be prosecuted. Conviction will follow unless the accused person can prove that the works were urgently necessary 'in the interests of safety or health, or for the preservation of the building', and that he told the planning authority what he had done as soon as possible afterwards.

In a serious case, the accused person can be tried at assizes or quarter sessions (or when the Courts Act 1971 comes into operation, the Crown Court). If he is convicted, he can be sentenced to up to twelve months' imprisonment and to a fine of unlimited amount. 'In determining the amount of any fine to be imposed on a person convicted on indictment, the court shall in particular have regard to any financial benefit which has accrued or appears likely to accrue to him in consequence of the offence.'

In addition to prosecuting the offender, the local planning authority may serve a listed-building enforcement notice on the owner of the building. A listed-building enforcement notice may demand that the owner restores the building to its former state, and if he fails to comply he may be prosecuted. Moreover the planning authority may do the necessary work and charge him with the cost of it.

Some buildings of special architectural or historic interest may not yet have been listed. If such a building appears to be in danger of demolition or of serious alteration, the planning authority may serve a 'building-preservation notice' on the owner or occupier. The building then enjoys the same protection as a listed building.[39]

A village or a county town may lose character even though all the important buildings are preserved. The charm of a village street may depend as much on the survival of relatively insignificant houses and cottages as on the preservation of more important buildings. Planning authorities have a duty to decide whether, for example, village streets or market squares need to be protected as a whole. Such groups of buildings are to be designated as 'conservation areas'. Special publicity must be given to all important planning applications in conservation areas so that as many people as possible are made aware of the applications and of their rights to make representations. Moreover the Secretary of State for the Environment or the Secretary of State for Wales[40] may direct planning authorities to take specified matters into consideration and to consult specified bodies when considering applications.[41]

The Secretary of State for the Environment may make grants towards the upkeep of 'buildings appearing to him to be of outstanding historic or architectural interest' the contents of the buildings, and adjacent land. A condition that the property is to be opened to the public at stated times may be imposed.[42]

national parks

Though in some countries, national parks are nationally owned, in Britain much of the land is owned by private persons. The Secretary of State for the Environment and the Secretary of State for Wales however have power, for the benefit of the public, to buy or take leases of land in national parks.

The parks are not administered by the Government but by joint boards or special committees to which the functions of the local planning authorities are delegated. The administering authorities have wide powers. To enable the public more readily to enjoy the beauties of the scenery, they may establish camping and picnic sites, build lavatories, and make car parks. If necessary they may buy land compulsorily for these purposes. They may arrange with local councils for motor traffic to be restricted. They can take steps to prevent open moorland from being ploughed. Some of these powers can be exercised in the countryside in general by the local planning authorities as well as by the special authorities in the national parks. Authorities may also promote sports in the national parks, encouraging, for example, sailing on the lakes and fishing in the rivers.

Bylaws may be made to ensure that visitors behave in an orderly manner and with consideration for others. To take one instance, it may be stipulated that motor boats on lakes are fitted with silencers to prevent excessive noise. Wardens may be appointed to ensure that the bylaws are observed.[43]

country parks, camping sites and picnic sites

Under the Countryside Act 1968,[44] local authorities may establish country parks. The idea is to provide opportunities for open-air recreation on a small scale fairly close to the large towns. Land for country parks may be acquired compulsorily.

Local authorities may also provide camping sites for holidaymakers and picnic sites for motorists and others using the roads.[45]

the green belt

The green belt was established in 1938 to restrict the further outward spread of London. There is green belt land in Buckinghamshire, Essex, Hertfordshire, Kent, Surrey, and Greater London.

The local authorities within that area may acquire land for the green belt, and they may also add privately owned land to the green belt by agreement with landowners. Plans showing green belt land have to be deposited with the Secretary of State for the Environment. Generally speaking, green belt land cannot be built upon, and land cannot be taken out of the green belt, without permission.

Planning authorities have established green belts round certain other cities and large towns. These green belts are, however, protected by the town and country planning legislation and not by the green belt legislation. In a sense, therefore, they are unofficial. The only green belt recognised by law is London's.[46]

access to the countryside

Local planning authorities have a duty to take steps to enable the public to have access to open country for open-air recreation. Open country was originally defined as any area appearing to the local planning authority to 'consist wholly or predominantly of mountain, moor, heath, down, cliff, or foreshore'. Recently, however, the definition has been made wider, and it now includes woodlands, rivers and canals not owned or managed by the British Waterways Board, and 'any expanse of water through which a river or some part of the flow of a river runs', other than a public reservoir. In the case of rivers, canals, and lakes, towpaths, lakeside paths, and suitable places for picnics are also covered.

Planning authorities must survey all the open country in their areas so that they can decide to which parts the public ought to be allowed access. They must have regard to all the relevant circumstances, including the extent to which landowners are likely voluntarily to allow access, and the extent to which better facilities are needed. Where the land is in a national park or an area of outstanding natural beauty, planning authorities must consult the Countryside Commission before taking any action.

Action may take three forms. Land may be bought compulsorily in order that the public should have access to it. Alternatively without buying the land, the planning authority may make an access agreement with the landowner. If agreement is found to be impossible an access order may be made. Orders have to be confirmed by the Secretary of State for the Environment or the Secretary of State for Wales[47] before they come into operation. Planning authorities usually make some payment to the landowner in return for an access agreement, and if an access order is made, he is entitled to compensation.

Visitors who 'for the purpose of open-air recreation' enter land which is subject to an access agreement or an access order cannot be treated as trespassers unless they do damage, for example, to walls, hedges, fences, or gates. Landowners must do nothing to hinder access. Access may, however, be suspended by order of the Secretary of State for the Environment or the Secretary of State for Wales[48] at times when the ground is so dry that there is a serious risk of fire. Certain areas, principally land used for agriculture other than rough grazing, and the parks of country houses, may be specifically excepted from agreements and orders, and the public has no right to enter them.

Planning authorities must keep maps showing land which has been acquired for access or which is the subject of access agreements or access orders. Maps must also show, in the case of agreements and orders, what land has been excepted. Owners may display copies at entrances to land and local planning authorities may contribute towards the costs of display.[49]

Scotland

The law is similar to the law of England and Wales. The main Acts are the Town and Country Planning (Scotland) Act 1947, and the Town and Country Planning (Scotland) Act 1969. The functions of the Secretary of State for the Environment are carried out in Scotland by the Secretary of State for Scotland.

Northern Ireland

Two Acts form the basis of planning control in Northern Ireland. They are the Planning and Housing Act (Northern Ireland) 1931, and the Planning (Interim Development) Act (Northern Ireland) 1944. Responsibility for town and country planning is shared between the Ministry of Development and local authorities. The legislation is, in general, similar to that in England and Wales, but there are some differences.

The Ministry of Development may take action under the Amenity Lands Act (Northern Ireland) 1965 to remove eyesores. Where a site is derelict, the ministry may either acquire it, or help the owner to improve it. Local authorities have power to deal with 'unsightly and dilapidated structures' on any land within their areas.

There is no legislation similar to the Caravan Sites Act 1968. The paragraphs on gypsies therefore do not apply to Northern Ireland.

Notes to this chapter are on pages 184-6.

3 Other Official Bodies

Many national and local organisations do important work in the countryside. Some of these organisations are official bodies whose constitution and powers and duties are governed by statute. Others, however, are private organisations which are outside the scope of this book.

the National Trust

The National Trust for Places of Historic Interest or National Beauty was founded in 1895 by a number of people who believed that action was needed to prevent the countryside from being spoiled. It was re-incorporated under an Act of Parliament known as the National Trust Act 1907, which has been amended and added to by later National Trust Acts. The National Trust is, however, entirely independent of the state.

In the early days, the main object of the National Trust was to preserve places of particular beauty in the countryside for the benefit of the public. In the National Trust Act 1937, however, more emphasis was placed on the acquisition of buildings of architectural or historic interest and their contents, and upon the opening of them to the public.

The National Trust has power to acquire properties either by purchase or by gift. Properties accepted by the Inland Revenue in payment of estate duty may be transferred to the National Trust. It may make bylaws for the protection of its properties and for the good conduct of visitors and it may charge admission fees of a reasonable amount. Certain commons and other land to which the public had a right of access

41

at the time of acquisition, however, must be opened free.

When the National Trust accepts a house and leases it back to the former owner, the lease must normally contain certain covenants, one being that the public is to be admitted to the property at agreed times. Another covenant provides that the property is to be maintained in its present character.

The National Trust may also protect land without acquiring it. If a public-spirited owner wishes to preserve his property from unsightly development for the benefit of posterity, he may, if the National Trust agrees, make a covenant with it that the use of his land shall be restricted in a specified manner.[1] The wording of the covenant is important, and must be clear and unambiguous. In the unfortunate case of *National Trust v Midlands Electricity Board*[2] the judge decided that the covenant was so vague as to be almost meaningless.

The National Trust owned Midsummer Hill in the Malvern Hills. The Church Commissioners owned Castlemorton Common near Midsummer Hill. The Church Commissioners had made a covenant with the National Trust which said that 'no act or thing shall be done or placed or permitted to remain upon the land which shall injure, prejudice, affect, or destroy the natural aspect and condition of the land'. The electricity board wished to erect electricity poles on Castlemorton Common. The National Trust objected to the erection of the poles on the ground that they would spoil the view from Midsummer Hill, and tried to enforce the covenant. Giving judgement for the board, Mr Justice Vaisey said:

'It would be difficult to find wider, vaguer, and more indeterminate words than these . . . Who is to say what is to be the criterion . . . of an alteration of the natural aspect and condition of the land? . . . It is no doubt easy to suggest some acts or things which would come within the prohibition – if, for example the land were ploughed up or turned into a car park or building estate.

' The difficulty here is to ascertain the limits of the prohibited acts. The burning of bracken, for instance, would I should have thought obviously affect the aspect and condition of the land. During the hearing, counsel for the National Trust was driven to admit that the placing of a basket for litter on a short pole or a seat or a bench would amount to a breach of the condition. The prohibition is so vague that it is really impossible of apprehension . . . and in my judgement it is wholly unenforceable.'

The judge added that 'the nearest of these poles to Mid-summer Hill is at least 1,100 yards distant from it. No doubt the poles are visible from Midsummer Hill on a reasonably clear day, but the effect of their presence or absence from the landscape must be quite infinitesimal.'

So long as the covenant is clear and definite, the National Trust has a right to enforce it, though it must act promptly to stop all infringements. In the case of *Gee v National Trust*[3] the National Trust lost its right to enforce a covenant because it had been lax in the past. In 1938, a Mrs Hext, who owned about 300 acres of land towards the head of the Helford River in Cornwall, made a covenant with the National Trust that 'no building shall at any time be erected on any part of the land except such . . . buildings as shall reasonably be required for proper farming, cultivation, management, or enjoyment, or to increase the amenities of the estate including the mansion house and gardens.' During the next quarter of a century, however, the National Trust did permit quite a number of houses and other buildings to be erected near the river.

In 1963, Gee bought a house with three-quarters of an acre of land on the estate. He wanted to build another house on the plot, and applied for planning permission. Permission was refused by the local planning authority, but granted on appeal by the Minister of Housing and Local Government. The report of the inspector said that the house had been designed by a distinguished architect and that the site offered great scope and challenge for an interesting architectural scheme. The house would not be obtrusive as it was fairly well screened by trees. It would fit in with the riverside development. Gee asked the National Trust to relax the covenant in his favour. It refused, probably because it thought that enough development had taken place already. Gee applied to the Lands Tribunal, which has power to alter covenants, asking that the restrictions on building should be removed or modified. The Lands Tribunal refused to alter the covenant, and Gee appealed to the Court of Appeal.

Lord Denning declared: 'I am prepared to accept the view that the National Trust, under a covenant of this kind, is entitled to enforce it so as to protect the interests of which it is the custodian in this country. It is, under the statue, the custodian of the natural beauty of our land, the cliffs and downs, fields and woods, rivers and shores, and of the stately homes, historic buildings, cottages and barns. In respect of any inquiry to its interest as custodian of our natural beauty, I think it would be qualified to insist on this covenant.'

It had however already relaxed the covenant for the benefit of other people. Moreover, Lord Denning continued, 'this one house will fit snugly into this small wooded valley. It should architecturally be a pleasing feature. It will not do any damage to the amenities or beauty of the district.' The appeal succeeded.

Once property has been transferred to the National Trust, it normally remains the property of the trust in perpetuity. It is not, however, exempt from compulsory purchase if for example, a motorway is being constructed.

the Nature Conservancy

The Nature Conservancy was established by royal charter in 1949, but it is now a component body of the Natural Environment Research Council whose members are appointed by the Ministry of Education and Science. The Nature Conservancy gives advice on the conservation of animals and plants in Great Britain, and also sets up and manages nature reserves. It receives Government grants and its activities are mentioned in the annual report of the council which is laid before Parliament.

A nature reserve is an area of land which is specially managed so that plants and animals, and is some cases geographical features, may be studied and preserved. The Nature Conservancy may itself establish nature reserves, and may help local authorities and others in establishing them. It may acquire land compulsorily for this purpose.

Agreements between the Nature Conservancy and other persons or bodies for the establishment of nature reserves may provide that the cost is to be met wholly or partly by the Nature Conservancy. If the value of land is reduced by the imposition of restrictions on the use of it, compensation may be paid.

The Nature Conservancy may make bylaws for nature reserves, prohibiting or restricting the entry of people, animals, vehicles, or boats into or in the reserve. They may forbid the killing or disturbing of any living creatures or their eggs, interference with plants or soil, the lighting of fires, or the deposit of litter or rubbish.[4]

the Ancient Monuments Board

The Secretary of State for the Environment and the Secretary of State for Wales must appoint an Ancient Monuments Board[5] to give them advice on the preservation of ancient monuments and also to give free advice to owners on the treatment of monuments. The board may, however, call upon owners to pay their out-of-pocket expenses.

Certain bodies interested in the preservation of ancient monuments are represented on the board; these include the Royal Commission on Historic Monuments in England, the Royal Commission on Historic Monuments in Wales, the Society of Antiquaries of London, the Royal Academy of Arts, the Royal Institute of British Architects, the Trustees of the British Museum, and the Ministry of Education.[6]

Separate bodies may be constituted for England and Wales. The board or boards must send annual reports to the Secretary of State for the Environment or in the case of the Welsh board to the Secretary of State for Wales.[7] The reports must be laid before Parliament.[8]

the Historic Buildings Council

The Secretary of State for the Environment and the Secretary of State for Wales also appoint Historic Buildings Councils for England and Wales to advise them how to exercise their powers in connection with the preservation of buildings of outstanding historical or architectural interest and their contents. The members are appointed by the appropriate Secretary of State.[9]

The councils must send annual reports to the Secretary of State on all matters on which they have advised him during the preceding year. The reports must be laid before Parliament.[10]

country houses

The Historic Buildings Council may advise the Secretary of State for the Environment that the owner of a castle or country house should receive a grant for its maintenance. If a grant is made, the owner may be compelled to open the building to the public at stated times, and to charge specified entrance fees.

Many owners, however, open their houses to the public voluntarily. There is nothing to stop them from doing so. They are entitled to charge such admission fees and to make such rules for the conduct of visitors as they see fit. They can turn away persons who appear undesirable, so long as they do not discriminate on racial or other similar grounds. If a visitor causes damage, for example by defying a 'do not touch' notice and knocking down a valuable piece of porcelain, the owner may sue him for compensation in the courts.

parish churches

The parish church is often the focal point of the village which it serves. Sometimes, however, the village has disappeared, or moved away, and the church is left alone in the fields. Occasionally, it stands in the park of the manor house. Wherever it is, the parish church is usually an important feature of the landscape.

A parish church and its fittings is under the control of the incumbent, though the descendants of the people who erected monuments in the church may have certain rights to them. The incumbent is in charge of the keys of the church, and he is not bound to admit any person other than his own parishoners who wish to attend services.

The parochial church council in most cases is liable to keep the parish church in repair. Repair includes such matters as the replacing of broken windows, the re-paving of the floor when it becomes uneven, and the upkeep and fencing of the churchyard. The various dioceses have schemes for the periodic inspection of churches by architects. Persons doing damage in churches may be prosecuted under the criminal law.

In some parts of the country, the redistribution of population and the decline of religious observance have made certain churches redundant. Schemes for redundant churches are prepared by the Church Commissioners, and local planning authorities have no jurisdiction though they are kept informed of schemes. Draft schemes must be published in one or more local newspapers, and the schemes themselves have to be submitted for approval to the Privy Council.

When preparing schemes, the Church Commissioners must consult the bishop and the Advisory Board for Redundant Churches. The members of the advisory board are appointed by the Archbishops of Canterbury and York after consultation with the Prime Minister and the First Lord of the Treasury. The board gives information to the Church Commissioners about the historic or architectural qualities of redundant churches. It advises whether a church should be demolished, turned to another use, or preserved as a church. The board makes annual reports to the Archbishops of Canterbury and York, and copies of the reports are laid before the Church Assembly.

Every diocese has its own Redundant Churches Committee which helps the board and has the duty to make every endeavour to find suitable alternative uses for any redundant church in its area. If another use can be found, the scheme may provide for appropriation to that use. A church at Winchester, for example, has been turned into a theatre. A church at Chichester has become a bookshop, and a church at Norwich is now a museum. If no alternative use can be found, the scheme may provide for the demolition of the church.

When, however, a church is of such historic or architectural importance, that in the interests of the nation and the Church of England it ought to be preserved, and yet no other use for it can be found, the scheme may provide for care and maintenance by a body called the Redundant Churches Fund. The members of the fund are appointed by the Queen on the advice of the Archbishops of Canterbury and York. It receives money from the Church Commissioners and other donors, and spends it on suitable buildings, making annual reports on its work which are laid before Parliament.[11]

When alterations in the structure or furnishings of any church or churchyard which is in use are proposed, a faculty must be obtained from the bishop of the diocese. An application is made to the consistory court where the chancellor of the diocese acts for the bishop by delegation. Faculties are required, for example, for the putting in or removal of a window, for the installation of electric light or a heating system, and for the moving of pews or a font from one part of the church to another. A faculty is needed if the exterior of the church is to be altered in any way.

The consistory court has complete discretion whether or not to grant a petition for a faculty. The court is guided by the wishes of persons who are interested or affected, as well as by doctrinal, liturgical, and architectural or artistic considerations. Appeal from the decision of a consistory court may be made to the appropriate provincial court, Canterbury or York, and from the provincial court to the Judicial Committee of the Privy Council. The High Court may grant an injunction to prevent a church or churchyard from being altered without the authority of a faculty.[12]

In re St Edburga's, Abberton,[13] is a fairly recent case involving a faculty. It was heard by the Court of Arches, which is the Provincial Court of Canterbury. The Minister of Aviation had petitioned Worcester Consistory Court for a faculty to remove the spire of Abberton parish church, which was close to an airfield. The chancellor of the diocese had refused to grant the faculty on the ground that the risk of serious danger was insufficient to justify the removal of the spire. The minister appealed.

In giving judgment, Sir Henry Willink, QC, Dean of Arches, said that 'to make so substantial an alteration in the structure of a church is a serious matter for the justification of which there must be weighty grounds . . . Though the church is not ancient – it was entirely rebuilt in 1881 – the removal of the spire was strongly opposed . . . Spires are rare in Worcestershire and this spire is a very pleasing feature of the landscape'. But, he went on, 'the spire is directly in line with the runway just over two miles from the point at which aircraft flying in from the north-east should touch down. Measured from this point, the angle to the top of the spire is one in forty four . . . At no airfield should there be, in principle, an obstacle increasing the approach angle beyond one in fifty. The petitioner's proposal in this case would reduce the approach angle to one in fifty five . . . I came to the conclusion that the spire gives rise to a real and not a fanciful risk of a most serious disaster and that this risk could be valuably reduced by giving the petitioner the faculty for which he asks.' The faculty was granted.

Scotland

The National Trust for Scotland exercises functions similar to those of the National Trust in England and Wales. The Secretary of State for Scotland appoints the Ancient Monuments Board for Scotland on which the Royal Commission on the Ancient and Historical Monuments of Scotland is represented. The Secretary of State for Scotland also appoints a Historic Buildings Council for Scotland.

Northern Ireland

The National Trust has a Northern Ireland committee, and it is active there, as well as in England and Wales. An ancient monuments advisory committee advises the Ministry of Finance about monuments which should be preserved because they are of national importance. These monuments may include redundant churches. Under section 25 of the Irish Church Act 1869 the ministry may assist in the maintenance and upkeep of redundant churches.

The Church of Ireland was disestablished in 1869 and the ecclesiastical courts no longer have any jurisdiction in matters affecting the public.

Notes to this chapter are on page 186.

4 Living Things

Taking a valuable cultivated plant or a pet rabbit without permission is theft. Wild animals and wild plants, however, can be stolen only in certain circumstances. How far can a landowner regard a hare which runs wild on his land like his dog as his own? Do the primroses in his woods belong to him?

Under the Theft Act 1968, which applies in England and Wales only, a person steals 'when he is not in possession of the land and appropriates anything forming part of the land by severing it or causing it to be severed, or after it has been severed'. This means that a trespasser who goes into a wood and takes away branches for firewood is a thief. If the rule were not qualified it would mean than any person who picked wild flowers or gathered blackberries on private land would also be committing a criminal offence, so the Act goes on to say that 'a person who picks mushrooms growing wild on any land, or who picks flowers, fruit or foliage from a plant (which includes a shrub or tree) growing wild on any land, does not . . . steal what he picks unless he does it for reward or for sale or other commercial purpose'. So it all depends on the motive of the picker. If he picks primroses in order to decorate his house, he does not commit an offence, but if he picks with a view to selling them at the street corner or to a local florist, he is guilty of theft.

Wild creatures are to be regarded as property. But 'a person cannot steal a wild creature not tamed nor ordinarily kept in captivity, or the carcase of any such creature, unless it has been reduced into possession.' Hares running wild are not 'reduced into possession' and cannot be stolen. Game birds and chicks kept in pens or under wire, however, are reduced into possession. They are property, and the taking of them without permission is, therefore, theft. But when birds are set free, they cease to be in the possession of anybody. A person killing or capturing a wild creature at large cannot be convicted of theft, but he may be convicted of some other crime such as poaching, or an offence against the laws protecting certain animals and birds[1] (see Chapter 5).

cruelty to animals

The Protection of Animals Acts apply to all domestic animals and also to wild animals kept in captivity. They do not apply to wild animals which are at liberty.

It is an offence to cruelly beat, kick, ill-treat, over-drive, torture, infuriate, terrify or poison any animal protected by the Acts, or to cause such an animal to be so treated. It is also an offence of cruelty to cause unnecessary suffering to an animal by omitting to do something which ought to be done, or to transport an animal in such a manner as to cause unnecessary suffering.

In general, an intention to commit cruelty need not be proved. The offence is causing pain and suffering without good reason. In one old case, sawing off the horns of cattle close to their heads for the purpose of slightly increasing their value and for convenience in feeding and packing them in cattle vans was held to be unjustifiable and unnecessary, and therefore, to be cruelty. On the other hand, in another old case, the branding of lambs on the nose with a hot iron was held not to be cruelty, since it was reasonably necessary for their identification.

It is not cruelty to course or hunt a captive animal unless the animal is liberated in an injured, mutilated, or exhausted condition.

A person who is convicted of cruelty to an animal may be fined or imprisoned. In addition, the court may order the animal to be taken away from him. On a second or subsequent conviction of cruelty, he may be disqualified from keeping animals for such period as the court thinks fit.[2]

traps

In general, it is an offence to use a spring trap for the purpose of killing hares or rabbits, except in a rabbit hole. In certain circumstances, however, county agricultural executive committees may grant licences to use spring traps more widely. Traps must be of a type approved by the Ministry of Agriculture, Fisheries and Food and must be inspected daily.[3]

riding schools and stables

Any person keeping a riding school must obtain a licence from the local authority. In country districts, the local authority for this purpose is the county council. Premises may be inspected by local authorities.

It is an offence to keep a riding establishment without a licence, or to fail to comply with any condition in a licence. It is an offence to let out or use a horse for instruction when it is in such a condition that riding would be likely to cause it suffering. It is also an offence to let a horse out with defective equipment which is likely to cause it suffering or which may cause an accident to the rider.[4]

kennels and catteries

Any person keeping a boarding establishment for dogs or cats must obtain a licence from the local authority. When granting licences, local authorities must ensure that the premises are suitable and that the animals will be properly cared for. Licences must contain conditions as to housing and care. Premises may be inspected by local authorities. It is an offence to keep a boarding establishment without a licence or to fail to comply with conditions in a licence.[5]

protection of birds

The Protection of Birds Acts 1954-67 restrict the killing

of wild birds and the taking of their eggs. It is an offence wilfully to kill or injure or to attempt to kill or injure many wild birds, though it may be a defence that the birds were killed to preserve crops from damage. It is also an offence in many cases to damage or destroy eggs. In respect of some birds, it is even an offence to disturb them on or near their nests.

Birds like the eagle, the barn owl, the peregrine, the whooper swan, Bewick's swan, and the bearded and crested tit, are specially protected all the year. Other birds, including several species of wild duck, are specially protected in the close season. Offences against specially protected birds are more heavily punished than offences against other birds.

Certain birds, such as the woodcock, grouse, the snipe, certain species of wild goose, and certain species of wild duck may not be shot in the close season, but may be killed during the remainder of the year. Close seasons vary somewhat but normally fall within the period 1 February to 30 September (see page 67).

Birds which are thought to do damage, on the other hand, for example crows, rooks, gulls, magpies and house-sparrows may be killed by authorised persons at any time, and their eggs may be taken by anybody. Authorised persons include the owners and occupiers of land.

The police have power without warrant to stop and search persons whom they find committing offences, or whom they suspect to have committed offences. Persons failing to give names and addresses may be arrested.[6]

keepers of animals

The keeper of an animal has a general duty to ensure that the animal does not cause damage or injury. 'A person is a keeper of an animal if he owns the animal or has it in his possession or if he is the head of a household of which a member under the age of sixteen owns the animal or has it in his possession.' Suppose a father or a widowed mother gives a pet to a child of fifteen. The parent is liable as the keeper of the animal, even though the child has complete responsibility for looking after it.[7]

animals of a dangerous species

Animals are divided into two classes, those which belong to a dangerous species and those which do not. A dangerous species is one 'which is not commonly domesticated in the British Islands, and whose fully grown animals normally have such characteristics that they are likely unless restricted to cause damage or that any damage they may cause is likely to be severe'. Most animals which are kept in country zoos and safari parks fall into the dangerous class.

The general rule is that the keeper of an animal which belongs to the dangerous class is liable for any damage or injury caused by the animal. The keeper, however, is not liable if the damage or injury is due solely to the fault of the sufferer as where, for example, a man is fool enough to put his hand into the cage of a tiger as a zoo. Again the keeper is not liable when the sufferer has voluntarily accepted the risk. If an adult goes on a safari in the park of a country house and is mauled by a lion, the keeper might possibly be able to escape liability under this exception,[8] but he would almost certainly be liable for an injury to an unaccompanied child.

animals of a harmless species

The keeper of an animal of a harmless species may be liable for damage or injury caused by the animal if he knows or ought to know that the particular animal is likely to be dangerous. All domestic animals, bulls, cows, sheep, pigs, goats, horses, dogs and cats are of a harmless species. A man who is bitten by a dog, for example, will be entitled to damages only if the owner knew or should have known that the dog had already bitten, or had already attempted to bite a human being.[9]

In the case of *Fitzgerald v A. D. Cooke Bourne (Farms) Ltd and George Bateman*[10] the Court of Appeal decided that the owners of a horse which was merely playful, and not dangerous, were not bound to take any special precautions to protect the public. In that case, Mrs Fitzgerald was walking along a public footpath through a field near Bourne in Lincolnshire. Suddenly two young horses appeared and pranced up to and around her. One of them accidentally struck her with its shoulder and she fell down. She was not seriously injured, but she was frightened and afterwards she suffered from a nervous breakdown.

The horses were being trained for racing and Mrs Fitzgerald sued the company which owned the horses, and Bateman the groom who was employed to look after them. She claimed damages for personal injuries on the ground, amongst others, that the owners and the groom knew, or ought to have known, that the horse which had knocked her down was a dangerous animal. Two witnesses gave evidence for Mrs Fitzgerald. One witness said that his wife, who was pregnant at the time, and he had been walking through the field a few days before the accident. The horses had galloped towards them, and pranced round. His wife was scared and had taken refuge amongst some trees at the side of the footpath. He had been afraid that she might have lost the baby.

The other witness was the secretary of the Burghley Hunt, a man who as a trainer had a lifelong experience of horses. He said that the horses were being playful, and that he would expect playful behaviour from young horses of that kind. He thought it was undesirable to put them in a field through which a public footpath ran.

The case for the company and Bateman was that the horses were docile. They had been kept in the field in the daytime for some months before and after the accident, and had been regularly fed by local school children. They were led to and fro every day along a busy road from the farm to the field and there had never been any trouble.

The Court of Appeal rejected Mrs Fitzgerald's claim. Lord Justice Willmer said that the horse had merely a propensity to be playful. 'It was not evincing any hostility or being in any way offensive; it was conducting nothing in the nature of an attack on human beings crossing the field . . . It seems to me that it would be too much to expect that an ordinarily careful owner of horses should refrain from keeping them in a field because there is a chance that one of the horses in a playful mood might (as unfortunately happened in this case) come in contact with and injure someone lawfully walking along the highway.'

When a domestic animal, for example a bull or a dog, is really vicious, the keeper must ensure that it cannot harm members of the public. A trespasser, however, normally has no legal right to complain if he is attacked and injured, unless the animal attacking him was a guard dog, and it was unreasonable for the owner to keep a guard dog.[11]

bees

It seems that the owner of bees may be liable if the bees escape and sting a neighbour. The decision in an Irish case, *O'Gorman v O'Gorman*[12] would probably be followed in a modern English case where the facts were similar.

Patrick O'Gorman and Michael O'Gorman had two farms next door to each other in County Clare. Michael kept bees and had about twenty hives against his boundary fence, which adjoined the farmyard of Patrick. Patrick had complained to Michael two or three times when the bees had swarmed. On one occasion, Patrick's farm workers had been compelled to stop haymaking. On another occasion, Patrick himself had been attacked whilst digging potatoes.

On the day in question, Patrick was harnessing a horse in the farmyard at a time when Michael was smoking his bees out in order to collect the honey. A swarm of bees came over the boundary fence, and settled on the horse, and on Patrick and stung them both. The horse bolted and Patrick's foot was caught in the reins. He was thrown against the wall of the farmyard and was badly injured. Shortly afterwards, he died of his injuries.

Patrick's family brought a legal action against Michael, claiming damages for Patrick's death. They claimed that Michael 'wrongly, negligently, and injuriously kept on his land a swarm of bees, well knowing that the said bees were of dangerous and mischievous nature and accustomed to sting mankind and domestic animals.'

In court, Michael said in cross examination that he knew

that smoking bees out caused danger to people in the immediate vicinity. He admitted that he himself had taken precautions against the viciousness of the bees. He had covered his hands, and had thrown a cloak over his body.

Patrick's family won their case. Mr Justice Kenny said that 'the bees were kept in unreasonable numbers at an unreasonable place, and with appreciable danger to the occupants of the plaintiff's farm. Further, the honey was not taken with reasonable care, skill and prudence'.

damage to property

Animals sometimes stray and cause damage to property. If they stray on to neighbouring land, the owner is normally liable to pay compensation to the person who has suffered loss. He would have a defence only if he could prove that the neighbour was under a legal obligation to fence his property and had failed to do so.

A landowner may detain livestock not under the control of any person and on his land, provided that he gives notice to the police and to the farmer, if he knows who the farmer is, within forty-eight hours. Unless the farmer pays for the damage and for the expenses of keeping the livestock within twenty-one days, the landowner may sell the livestock.[13]

If cattle are being driven along a road and stray inadvertently into neighbouring gardens or fields, however, the rule is different. The farmer is not liable for any damage which the cattle may cause. If the owner of the house or the land wishes to prevent intrusion from the road he must put up a wall or a fence.[14]

In the case of *Tillett v Ward*[15] a farmer had bought a bull at Stamford market, in Lincolnshire. He was driving the bull through the streets of the town when it went through an open door into a shop and did a considerable amount of damage to the goods in the shop. The shopkeeper sued the farmer, but the court said that the farmer was not liable. The shopkeeper should have kept his door shut.

accidents on the road

Until recently, a farmer or the owner of a dog was not liable if his animal strayed on to the road and caused an accident. This was quite unfair, as the case of *Ellis v Johnstone*[16] showed.

Johnstone lived in a house in Chorley Wood Common Road, near Rickmansworth in Hertfordshire. The gate from the garden to the road was hardly ever closed. Johnstone owned a large Welsh collie dog which was in the habit of crossing over the road to the common quite frequently, and it had no road sense. Johnstone knew of this habit and had never attempted to train the dog, though the road was often busy.

On a November evening in 1960, Ellis was driving along Chorley Wood Common Road. As he approached the gate to Johnstone's house the dog dashed out and bounded across the road in the direction of the common. Ellis had no time to stop. His car struck the dog and killed it. The car was badly damaged, and he sued Johnstone, claiming the cost of repair.

Ellis lost his case in the Court of Appeal, though the judges were obviously sympathetic towards him. Lord Justice Donovan said that 'the occupier of land despite modern conditions of traffic is still under no liability at common law to prevent his domestic animals from straying on to the highway.' This rule has since been changed. Keepers of animals must now 'take such care as is reasonable to see that damage is not caused by animals straying on to a highway.' In judging whether reasonable care has been taken in a particular instance, factors to be taken into account probably include how busy the road is, and whether drivers are likely to be aware of the presence of animals. However, 'a person is not to be regarded as committing a breach of the duty to take care by reason only of placing animals on any common land or town or village green or land situated in an area where fencing is not customary in any case where he has a right to do so.'[17]

dogs and livestock

The keeper of a dog which worries livestock (other than

Living Things

livestock which has strayed on to his land), is guilty of an
offence. A magistrates' court may order the dog to be
destroyed if it does not appear to be kept under proper control.
Worrying means attacking or chasing livestock in such a way
as may reasonably be expected to cause injury or suffering
to them or loss of milk or eggs.[18] In addition to his criminal
responsibility, the keeper of the dog is liable to pay for the
losses.[19]

Persons who have a right to 'act for the protection of livestock' may kill or injure a stray dog which is endangering
livestock. A person has the right to 'act for the protection of
livestock' when he is the owner of the livestock, the owner or
occupier of the land where the livestock is kept, or a person
authorised by one of these people. Such a person is entitled
to act when he has a reasonable belief than one of two conditions is fulfilled. One condition is 'that the dog is worrying
or is about to worry the livestock and there are no other
reasonable means of ending the worrying'. The alternative
condition is 'that the dog has been worrying livestock, has
not left the vicinity, and is not under the control of any person and there are no practicable means of ascertaining to
whom it belongs.'[20]

A person who kills, wounds, or maims a dog, even when
the dog is trespassing, commits an offence unless he 'acts for
the protection of livestock.'[21] A person committing the offence
is also liable to pay damages to the owner of the dog.

In the case of *Thayer v Newman*[22] the shooting of a dog
was held to be justified. A farmer had been suffering losses
because dogs had worried his sheep. He asked one of his men
to keep a look out for dogs. One morning the man saw two
dogs chasing a sheep, though apparently not in a ferocious
manner. The man shot one of the dogs, and the owner of the
dog sued him for damages.

The Court of Appeal decided that the action of the man
was justifiable and refused to award damages. Lord Denning
said that 'the chasing of sheep by a dog, whether done in play
or out of malice, is a real and serious menace against which a
farmer is entitled to protect himself by shooting the dog if that
is, in all the circumstances, a reasonable thing to do.'

In the case of *Workman v Cowper*,[23] however, the shooting was held to be unjustified. In that case, a foxhound had been living wild in and around Peppard Common in Oxfordshire for several weeks, during the winter of 1959-60. Unsuccessful attempts had been made to catch it. The area around Peppard Common was hunted by the South Berkshire hounds, but the hound did not belong to that pack. However, the master of the pack considered himself responsible for any hound, whether or not it came from his pack. He authorised Cowper to kill the hound if he could find it. Cowper discovered it asleep and believing that he could not catch it, shot it dead.

Cowper was charged with maliciously killing the dog. In evidence it was said that the lambing season was approaching, and that a stray dog could be expected to cause damage to livestock. However, no damage was known to have been done by this particular dog. The Henley on Thames justices decided that as Cowper had acted on the best possible authority, that of the master of the pack of hounds which hunted in the district, he had acted reasonably in all the circumstances. They dismissed the charge but the prosecution appealed.

The High Court ordered the case to be sent back to the justices with a direction to convict. Lord Parker said: ' It is clear that this hound presented no real and present danger to sheep and lambs, or any other animal. The most that can be said is that it might in the future chase sheep which were in lamb, or attack the lambs when born. But there was no indication at that point of time when the dog was shot that there was any real or imminent danger of that occurring. Accordingly . . . no lawful excuse has been shown . . . It is true . . . that the defendant got the best authority he could, namely, from the master of the South Berkshire hounds, but it is quite clear that there was no one who could give him authority to kill the dog.'

dog collars

The owner of a dog must ensure that his dog, whilst on a public highway, wears a collar. The name and address of the owner must be shown on the collar or on a plate attached to the collar. This rule does not apply to packs of hounds, to dogs used for sporting purposes, or for the destruction of vermin, or to farm dogs.[24]

dog licences

Dog licences must be obtained for all dogs over the age of six months which are not exempted. Guide dogs kept by the blind, and hounds under the age of twelve months which have never been used in a pack are exempted. The most important exemption, however, is for dogs kept and used solely for the purpose of tending sheep or cattle on a farm and by a shepherd for his sheep. Game licences as well as dog licences must normally be obtained when a dog is used for sport.

It is an offence to keep a dog without a licence, or to fail to produce a licence to the police or to any other authorised person within a reasonable time after request. Offenders may be prosecuted. Registers of dog licences must be kept by the clerk of the county council or the county borough council issuing them. A licence may be suspended after a conviction for cruelty.[25]

Except for certain farm animals (referred to on page 147) licences are not required for keeping other animals, even dangerous animals from overseas.

cats

The owner of a cat is not liable if the cat strays and causes damage. The leading case on cats is *Buckle v Holmes*.[26] Buckle and Holmes lived in the same road in Leeds, Buckle being a pigeon fancier who also kept chickens. One night, a cat owned by Holmes strayed into Buckle's garden and killed thirteen pigeons and two chickens. Buckle sued Holmes for damages, but the Court of Appeal refused to award them. Lord Justice Bankes said that a cat was a useful domestic animal. It could not ordinarily be kept shut up, Accordingly he concluded that 'it is impossible to hold the owner of a cat responsible for its trespass which results in damage to his neighbour's pigeons or poultry'.

sick animals

When an owner is aware that one of his animals is suffering from an infectious or a contagious disease, he has a duty to isolate it from animals owned by other persons. In particular, he must not take the animal to a cattle market. If he fails to isolate the animal, he is liable to other owners whose animals are affected. An owner who sells diseased animals with a guarantee that they are free from disease is liable for any damage caused whether or not he was aware of the disease.

Under the Diseases of Animals Act 1950, the owners of animals suffering from serious infectious or contagious diseases such, for example, as foot and mouth disease must give notice to the police who in turn must give notice to the Ministry of Agriculture, Fisheries and Food or to the local authority. Veterinary surgeons attending the animals have a similar duty.

The Ministry of Agriculture, Fisheries and Food may make orders declaring areas to be infected. The orders may prohibit or restrict the movement of human beings and animals into, in, and out of infected areas. The minister may also make orders for the slaughter of infected animals or of animals which have been in contact with infected animals, and for the seizure of carcases. Compensation must be paid to the owners.[27]

It is an offence deliberately to use a rabbit infected with myxomatosis to spread the disease among uninfected rabbits.[28]

Scotland

The Theft Act 1968 and the Animals Act 1971 do not apply to Scotland. The matters contained in these Acts are mostly covered by the common law of Scotland. The most important difference is that the owner of animals is normally under no liability if they stray on to the highway. Otherwise the common law does not differ greatly from the statutory law in England and Wales.

Northern Ireland

In Northern Ireland there is no legislation similar to the Riding Establishments Acts or the Animal Boarding Establishments Act. This means that riding schools and stables and kennels and catteries can be kept without licence.

The Animals Act 1971 does not extend to Northern Ireland, and the old common-law rules about animals still remain in force. The most striking peculiarity of the old law is that the owner of an animal is not liable if it strays on to the highway and causes injury to or damage to the property of a passer by. However, an Act similar to the Animals Act 1971 is likely to be passed soon by the Parliament of Northern Ireland.

Notes to this chapter are on pages 186-7.

5 Country Sports

The use of the countryside for recreation is bound to increase. The traditional sports, hunting, shooting, and fishing, are all flourishing. The newer sports, like sailing, increase in popularity. Hunting, shooting, fishing, and sailing are dealt with in this chaper. Walking and rambling are considered in the next chapter.

foxhunting

Foxes are wild animals which, unless they are kept as pets, are not subject to the laws against cruelty. There is no close season for foxhunting. So far as the law is concerned, foxes may be hunted all the year round.

Hunts do not enjoy any special right to enter private land. This was decided in the case of *Paul v Summerhayes*.[1] Summerhayes managed a farm on behalf of his father. Paul was a member of the hunt. A fox which was being pursued by the hunt ran into a field belonging to the farm. The hunt tried to enter the field, but Summerhayes warned them off. A scuffle developed, during which Summerhayes was slightly injured. He brought a private prosecution for assault against Paul and another member of the hunt. In the magistrates' court, they were convicted and fined.

The two men, however, appealed against conviction. They argued that foxes are harmful animals. The hunt was conferring a benefit on the public by destroying foxes, and so had a right to enter private property. The assault on Summerhayes was excusable, because it had taken place in the exercise of this right. The court did not accept this argument and dismissed the appeal. Lord Coleridge pointed out: 'The question is whether under the circumstances Summerhayes was justified in resisting the entry of the hunt on his father's land. I am of opinion that he was. It was suggested . . . that foxhunting . . . as a sport can be carried on over the land of a person without his consent and against his will . . . I am of the opinion that no such right as that claimed exists. The sport of foxhunting must be carried on in subordination to the ordinary right of property. Questions such as the present do not often arise, because those who pursue the sport of foxhunting do so in a reasonable spirit, and only go on the lands of those whose consent is expressly, or may assumed to be tacitly, given.'

On the other hand, if the trespass of the hunt is inadvertent, the courts look upon it with some tolerance. In the case of *Chamberlain v Sandeman*,[2] in the Haywards Heath County Court in 1965, the huntsman of the Crawley and Horsham Hunt was unable to call off the hounds, which chased a fox into the garden of some people called Chamberlain. Mr and Mrs Chamberlain took a great pride in their garden, and the hounds did a considerable amount of damage. The hunt was legally liable to pay the cost of putting the garden right, and it did not dispute this liability. Mr and Mrs Chamberlain, however, were not satisfied. They applied to the court for an injunction ordering the master of the hunt to stop keeping foxhounds. The judge refused to make the injunction: 'The plaintiffs, are fully justified in saying that they do not want hounds on their property. But foxhunting is a legal pastime under the law of England. Many farmers and landowners have no objection to the hunt passing over their land, and the hunt will always pay for damage done. The fox's escape route is unpredictable, and it is not always possible to call off the hounds. The plaintiffs had built their house in a quiet part of the Sussex countryside; the risk of incursion by hounds is a small price to pay for the escape from petrol fumes and roar and bustle of traffic and humanity. This is not a case for the issue of an injunction.'

licences for shooting

Generally speaking, game licences are required for shooting game and deer. In some circumstances, they are also required for shooting hares and rabbits. Firearm or shotgun certificates are also necessary.[3]

close seasons and days

For a large part of the year, it is an offence to shoot game or deer. Grouse may be shot between 12 August and 10 December. Partridges may be shot between 1 September and 1 February, and pheasants may be shot between 1 October and 1 February. The rest of the year is the close season. Sundays and Christmas Day are close days, even in the open season.

So far as deer are concerned, generally speaking it is an offence to kill males between 1 May and 31 July, and females between 1 March and 31 October. There are exceptions, however, for killing to prevent suffering and to prevent serious damage to crops.[4]

the right to shoot

The only person who has an absolute right to shoot during the open season is the owner on his own land. The owner may, however, authorise others to shoot on his land.

Where land is let without any mention of shooting rights they pass to the tenant automatically, except that the tenant must not shoot hares and rabbits at night. This exception does not apply when the shooting rights are given to the tenant expressly.

If the owner lets the shooting rights, and not the land itself, the tenant has an exclusive right to kill game birds on the land during the period of the lease, though the owner may kill hares and rabbits.

A landowner may let the land, but reserve the shooting rights for himself. This does not prevent the tenant from

67

shooting hares and rabbits, and any agreement which attempts to stop it is null and void.[5]

poaching game and rabbits

Persons who without any right or permission shoot game, birds, hares or rabbits or trespass with a view to shooting them, are poachers. Poaching is an offence which is more serious when there are five or more poachers together. Night-time poaching is generally speaking a more serious offence than day-time poaching.[6]

poaching deer

It is an offence without authority to take or kill deer, or to attempt to take or kill them. For a first offence, the poacher may be fined. The courts may impose a term of imprisonment for a second or subsequent offence.[7]

searching and arresting poachers

The police have power to stop and search suspected poachers, but a gamekeeper has no such power. The police have power to arrest poachers by day or night and a gamekeeper has power to arrest poachers by night so long as he himself is employed by the owner or tenant of the land, and not by a mere shooting tenant. Any gamekeeper, however, may arrest a poacher by day under certain circumstances. The circumstances are that the gamekeeper has asked the poacher for his name and address, and has asked him to leave, and the poacher has refused to give his name and address or has refused to leave. The Court of Criminal Appeal in the case of *R v Wilson*[8] decided that these requirements must be strictly observed.

Wilson was found by a gamekeeper poaching rabbits in a Nottinghamshire wood. The gamekeeper knew where Wilson lived but did not know his name. He therefore simply asked Wilson for his name. Wilson refused to give it, and the gamekeeper arrested him. Wilson made an unsuccessful attempt to get away. He kicked the gamekeeper and called to a second man to get out his knife. Wilson was subsequently charged by the police with 'assault with intent to prevent lawful apprehension'. The court, however, found him not guilty because the gamekeeper had not asked Wilson for his address. The apprehension, therefore, was not lawful.

The Court of Criminal Appeal reached its decision with obvious reluctance. 'Thus' said Lord Goddard 'arises one of those technicalities which it would be a good thing to have abolished, because very often a gamekeeper may know perfectly well where a person lives though he does not know his name.' The technicalities however still exist.[9]

interference with game

People who are shooting lawfully have a right to stop malicious interference with their shooting. They can use a reasonable amount of force, if necessary, even against persons on a public road. There is an old case about this, *Harrison v Duke of Rutland*.[10] The Duke of Rutland and his friends were shooting grouse on some moors across which a road ran. Harrison apparently had some kind of grudge against the duke. He stood on the road, waving his handkerchief, and opening and shutting his umbrella in order to scare the grouse away. The keepers told him to stop the nuisance, but he took no notice. The keepers therefore caught hold of him, and held him on the ground until the drive was over.

Harrison sued the duke, as employer of the keepers, for assault. The duke counterclaimed for damages for trespass. The court had no difficulty in deciding the case in favour of the duke. As Lord Justice Kay said, 'the plaintiff went upon this highway not for the purpose of exercising as one of the public his right of passage, but of interfering with the grouse drive . . . Such a nuisance on . . . the highway is trespass.'

The law, however, is not so favourable to sportsmen when the interference is caused by a dog, as the case of *Gott v Measures*[11] showed. Gott, who lived in Lincolnshire fen country near Spilsby, owned a black labrador bitch. The dog had a habit of trespassing on land over which Measures had the shooting rights. Measures frequently told Gott to keep his dog under control. Matters came to a head when Measures saw the dog tearing a hen pheasant to pieces on a dyke, and shortly afterwards saw it chasing a hare. He was so incensed that he went to fetch his gun. When he returned to see the dog chasing a second hare, he shot it dead.

Gott prosecuted Measures for unlawfully and maliciously killing his dog. Measures pleaded not guilty. His defence was that the killing was neither unlawful nor malicious. He had caught the dog in the act of killing one of his pheasants and of chasing two hares. He was entitled to kill the dog in order to safeguard his property. The Spilsby magistrates found that his act was justified and dismissed the charge. Gott appealed against the dismissal of the charge to the King's Bench Division and won his appeal. The court ordered the case to be sent back to the magistrates with a direction to convict Measures. Lord Goddard said that: 'Measures had no property in the game until he had reduced the game into possession. Neither a person owning the sporting rights, nor the landowner has any property in wild game. He has no property in a covey of partridges or in wild pheasants. If he has pheasants in breeding pens that is another matter, because they are in the same position as domestic fowls: but he has no property in a hare unless and until he has shot the hare and got it . . . It seems to me that you cannot honestly believe that it is necessary to shoot a dog to protect your property when you have no property to protect.'[12]

dead game

Game birds, hares, and rabbits are quite often killed accidentally by motor traffic on the road. If the bird or animal is killed on a private road through an estate, it is, to use a legal phrase 'reduced into possession', and becomes the property of the landowner. If the bird or animal is killed on a public road, it becomes the property either of the owner of the land beside the road, or of the highway authority which maintains the road. This is a difficult point of law which has not been finally settled. Whatever the true position, however, it seems that the passing motorist has no right to take dead game and may be guilty of theft if he does so.[13]

shooting over footpaths

There is no reason why people with shooting rights should not shoot over public footpaths which run across their land. They must, however, take great care not to create an obstruction and not to shoot so as to endanger members of the public. The right of the public is paramount, and people who shoot must not expect persons using a footpath to wait until a drive is over.

damage by game

When game escapes and does damage to crops, the person entitled to shooting rights on the land from which the game escaped, may have to compensate the farmer.

He will have to compensate the farmer if he released game in unreasonable numbers, as happened in the case of *Farrer v Nelson*.[14] Farrer had a farm on the Sizergh estate in Westmorland. Nelson had shooting rights over an eighty acre wood on the estate. Within a short period, Nelson set free in the wood 450 pheasants which he had reared elsewhere. In August 1884, the pheasants did a great deal of damage to the crops in a field farmed by Farrer; at one time, a hundred pheasants were seen running there. Farrer brought a legal action against Nelson.

Giving judgment, Baron Pollock said that 'as I understand the law, each person in this country is entitled to bring on his land any quantity of game which can reasonably and properly be kept on it.' The game which Nelson had released in the wood, however, exceeded that quantity. 'The moment he brings on game to an unreasonable amount or causes it to increase to an unreasonable extent, he is doing that which is unlawful, and an action may be maintained by his neighbour for the damage which he has sustained.'

On the other hand, if pheasants have increased in number through natural causes, and not through overstocking, there is no liability under the common law to pay compensation. This was decided in the case of *Seligman v Docker*.[15] Docker had a thousand acres of woodland at Crawley near Winchester. Seligman farmed nearby. The spring of 1947 was, so we are told, a wonderful season for breeding pheasants, and there were twice as many pheasants in the woods at the beginning of the 1947-8 season as there had been at the beginning of the 1946-7 season. During the autumn of 1947 and the spring of 1948, the pheasants caused a great deal of harm to crops on the farm. Seligman claimed damages.

Mr Justice Romer asked 'who was responsible for the presence in the autumn of 1947 of wild pheasants so much in excess of those which had been found in any previous year? I am satisfied that it was not due to any unreasonably large stock having been left after the close of the shooting season 1946-7 . . . The evidence which was given upon this point leads to one conclusion and one conclusion only and that is that it was due to exceptional weather conditions which prevailed in Hampshire, as elsewhere, in the summer of 1947 and particularly during the very important months of May and June.' Seligman lost his case.

There may, however, be a statutory obligation to pay compensation even when there is no obligation under the common law. Under the Agricultural Holdings Act 1948, the owners of agricultural land must pay compensation when the crops of their tenant farmers are damaged by game.[16]

fishing in the sea and tidal waters

The people of Britain have a right to fish freely in the sea up to six miles from the coast. This right is enjoyed to the exclusion of foreigners.[17] Generally speaking, the public is also free to fish in river estuaries and in tidal waters. There are, however, a few exceptions to the general rule. In particular, the owners of piers and jetties may charge fees for the privilege of using their property as a base from which to fish.

Tidal waters include rivers as far upstream as the tide runs. Whether particular waters are, or are not, tidal can be discovered by looking carefully at the appropriate sheet of the one-inch Ordnance Survey map. Tidal waters are edged with a black line. Waters which are not tidal are edged with a blue line. The point on the map where the black line gives way to the blue line is the place on the river beyond which the tide does not run.

fishing in non-tidal waters

On non-tidal stretches of river, the fishing rights are nearly always private. They usually belong to the owners of the land on the banks of the river, though sometimes they have been acquired by others. Private waters include streams, canals, and inland lakes and ponds. The fishing rights over them generally belong to the owners of the banks, shores, or surrounding land. In the case of a canal, the rights usually belong to the owners of the canal.

Members of the public are not entitled to fish in private waters unless they obtain a lease of the fishing rights, or the permission of the owner. If they fish without permission, they are liable to be sued for trespass by the owner in the civil courts,[18] or even to be prosecuted under the Theft Act 1968.[19]

In the case of *Harris v Earl of Chesterfield*,[20] the Earl of Chesterfield and a Mrs Foster brought proceedings against Harris and a man called Bailey. They alleged that Harris and Bailey had trespassed by fishing in the river Wye a few miles below Hereford. The earl owned land on one bank of the Wye, and Mrs Foster had land on the opposite bank. They argued that as owners of the banks of the river they had exclusive rights of fishing in the length of river which adjoins their lands. They said that Harris and Bailey, by fishing there, had infringed their rights.

Harris lived in the parish of King's Caple, and Bailey lived in the parish of Hentland. They produced evidence which showed that people living in five parishes along the Wye, including King's Caple and Hentland, had fished in the Wye for several centuries. There had never been anything surreptitious about the fishing, and the people who fished had never been challenged. Harris and Bailey asked the court to make a presumption, which is often made when a practice has gone on without challenge for many years. They asked the court to presume that, at some time in the Middle Ages, the king must have granted a right to their predecessors. In this case, they said, the king must have given a charter to the inhabitants of the five parishes, allowing them to fish in the Wye. The House of Lords refused to make such a presumption, Lord Gorell concluding that 'long as the defendants and their predecessors have fished these waters, they have not had a legal right to do so, although they have fished in the assertion of a right. Their action seems to have been more or less tolerated, but their rights have not been fully tested until this case.' The earl and Mrs Foster, therefore won their case.

The Theft Act 1968 creates two different offences, angling in the daytime, and any other kind of unlawful fishing. The second offence is the more serious, and in some circumstances the offender may be sent to prison. Using certain implements, poison, or an explosive to catch fish are offences under the Salmon and Freshwater Fisheries Acts 1923.

The case of *Wells v Hardy*[21] shows that even the most technical offence may be theft. Wells was the assistant secretary of the Fulham Angling Club. He had fished regularly in the Thames at Taplow for more than twenty years, and other people had fished there for forty years, without incident. Wells fished for sport only, releasing all the small fish at once and putting the rest in a net in the water, where they stayed until the end of the day and were then released. None of the fish ever came to any harm.

Without much warning, in 1964, Wells received a summons to attend the Burnham magistrates' court. He was charged with 'unlawfully and wilfully attempting to take fish in water, namely, the river Thames, in which there was a private right of fishing'. The private fishery was said to belong to Hardy. The river bank was reached by an unmade private road which ran almost parallel to the river. Hardy owned a house on the other side of this road, and proved to the satisfaction of the court that his land extended across the road to the river bank. So the magistrates' court convicted Wells and fined him a nominal sum. Wells appealed as a matter of principle. His counsel argued that he ought not to have been convicted of theft, as he had not had any intention of depriving the owner of the fish permanently. The court, however, decided that any taking of fish, whether permanently or not, was theft. The conviction had to stand.

close seasons for fishing

Close seasons for certain fish have been established. The close season for salmon generally lasts from the beginning of September to the end of January. The close season for trout is a month longer, from the beginning of September to the end of February. The close season for other freshwater fish is from 15 March to 15 June. Close seasons for different periods may, however, be established on any river by bylaws made by the river authority.

River authorities may also make bylaws to prohibit the capture of salmon and trout by commercial means, on certain days. If there are no bylaws, the prohibited time is at the weekend between six on Saturday morning and six on Monday morning.[22]

fishing licences

Licences for the fishing of salmon and trout are required, and for the catching of other fish may be required. Licences are issued by river authorities.[23]

boats

The public has a general right of navigation over the sea and over tidal waters. The right, however, has limits. A judge once described it as a 'right to pass and repass and to remain for a reasonable time' without being obstructed. Mooring for a 'reasonable time' probably means no longer than overnight or whilst stormy weather or a fog lasts. Ports and harbours and, in a few places, private persons, may charge a fee or a toll for anchoring or mooring.

There is, generally speaking, no right to land on the banks of a river except by necessity, and no right to use a path along the river bank for towing. The permission of the landowner must be obtained. Rights of landing and towing, however, may exist in certain places because the landowner has not raised any objection for twenty years or more, or by virtue of local customs.

In waters which are not tidal, there is no public right of navigation. The bed of the river belongs to the owner of the land which adjoins the river banks. If the land on each bank is separately owned, the boundary between the two properties runs down the middle of the river. The bed of a lake would also seem to belong to the proprietors of the land surrounding it, though the law on this point is not finally settled. The landowners can prevent the use of a boat on the water.

There are, however, many exceptions to the rule. In some waters which are not tidal, a public right of navigation does exist. It may have arisen because the public has been in the habit of using a river for a long period, or it may have been expressly granted by an Act of Parliament. The public has, for example, express rights to navigate on the Thames between Teddington and Cricklade subject to the bylaws made by the conservators of the River Thames.

Scotland

Close seasons, and days, for game and deer which are the same as in England and Wales, have been established by the Game (Scotland) Act 1832 and the Deer (Scotland) Act 1959. Persons who fish without permission are liable to be prosecuted for poaching.

Northern Ireland

A Fisheries Conservancy Board has been established. The board is responsible for the control of fishing in inland waters and for the issue of licences.[24]

Notes to this chapter are on pages 187-8.

6 Communications and Transport

A public highway may come into existence by dedication or by Act of Parliament. In the case of dedication the owner of land dedicates or is presumed to have dedicated, land to the public for the purpose of passage. Dedication is presumed when a right of way has been used by the public for twenty years without interruption, unless it is proved that there was no intention to dedicate during that period.[1]

Many main roads were built under the Turnpike Acts of the eighteenth and nineteenth centuries. Today, new roads in the country are constructed by the Secretary of State for the Environment and by county councils in their capacity as highway authorities. In the normal way, the highway below the surface of the road is owned by the owner of the adjoining land. Where the road divides two properties the boundary runs down the middle.[2]

the right of passage

The public has a right to use a public highway to travel from one place to another. In the case of bridle paths and footpaths the right is, of course, limited to certain kinds of traffic.

There is no right to linger on the highway unreasonably. It is reasonable to linger when there has been an accident, when a car has broken down, and for purposes reasonably incidental to the journey.

In the case of *Hickman v Maisey*[3] the Court of Appeal discussed the question of when lingering is and is not reasonable. Hickman owned land on the Wiltshire Downs which was crossed by a public road. The land was used for the training and trial of racehorses. Maisey forecast the performance of racehorses in a sporting paper and he was in the habit of watching the horses from the road. The trainer warned him off several times, but to no effect. On the day in question, Maisey walked backwards and forwards over a fifteen yard stretch of the road for about and hour and a half, observing the trial of horses through binoculars. Hickman brought proceedings against Maisey for trespass and for an injunction to stop him from trespassing in the future. Hickman claimed that the value of his land for the training of racehorses was diminished by the spying.

Lord Justice Smith said that the public had a right to use the highway for reasonable purposes. 'For instance, if a man, while using the highway for passage, sat down for a time to rest himself by the side of the road, to call that a trespass would be unreasonable. Similarly . . . if a man took a sketch from the highway, I should say that no reasonable person would treat that as an act of trespass. But I cannot agree . . . that the acts which this defendant did, not for the purpose of using the highway as such, but, for the purpose of carrying on his business as a racing tout to the detriment of the plaintiff by watching the trials of racehorses on the plaintiff's land, were within such an ordinary and reasonable use of the highway as I have mentioned.' The court awarded nominal damages, and granted an injunction to stop repetition of the trespass by Maisey.

maintenance of roads

The surface of a public road is normally owned by the highway authority, which is responsible for keeping the road in a reasonable state of repair. The highway authority for trunk roads is the Secretary of State for the Environment, and for other roads in the country is usually the county council. The liability to repair may be enforced by order of the appropriate quarter sessions (or by the Crown Court when the Courts Act 1971 comes into operation) after a complaint has been made.[4]

The maintenance of a private road is, of course, the responsibility of its owner or owners.

new roads

When the Secretary of State for the Environment proposes to build a motorway, he must publish a notice in at least one local paper in each area through which the new road is to run. The notice must give general information about the proposed route, and must state at what place or places a detailed map may be inspected.

The Secretary of State must send copies of the map to the council of each county and county borough or district which is affected by the proposals. The councils then have three months in which to make objections. Other persons may make objections to the Secretary of State within the same time limit.

When an objection is made by a council, the Secretary of State must hold a local inquiry. When an objection is made by a private person, however, he may refuse to hold an inquiry if he is 'satisfied that in the circumstances of the case an inquiry is unnecessary.' A private objector whose objection is not merely personal should, therefore, try to persuade his council to make an objection on his behalf. After an inquiry has been held, the Secretary of State has full power to confirm the plan with or without any modification as he pleases. The only fetter on his discretion is that he is obliged 'to give due consideration to the requirements of local and national planning including the requirements of agriculture.'[5]

Once a plan has been confirmed the owners of property in the line of the new motorway may be compelled to sell it. They need not, however, wait for compulsory-purchase notices to be served on them. If the value of their property has been diminished by the plan, which must almost invariably be the case, they may require the Secretary of State to buy it from them in advance.[6]

On a compulsory purchase, the owner is entitled to compensation for the land taken and for the reduction in value, if any, of the remainder of his property. The compensation for reduction in value, however, may not cover the full loss as the case of *Edwards v Minister of Transport*[7] showed. Edwards owned a house, with about four acres of land, at Albrighton in Shropshire. When a new trunk road from Birmingham to Birkenhead was built, a very small portion of his land was taken, the value of which was £50. At a point very close to his house, the new road was on a steep rise. He found that his property was badly affected by dust. Moreover at night he and his family were continually disturbed by the headlights of cars and lorries shining through his windows and the crashing of gears.

The compensation for reduction in value might be calculated in two ways. If the effect on his property of the whole of the new road were taken into account, the proper compensation would have been £4,000. If, however, the compensation had to be limited 'to the damage suffered by the claimant from acts done on the two small pieces of land which the minister had acquired from him' the figure would be £1,600 only. The Lands Tribunal assessed the compensation at the higher amount. The minister appealed and the Court of Appeal decided reluctantly that the lower figure was correct. Lord Justice Donovan said:

'If a public authority acting upon statutory powers constructs a highway opposite my house but takes none of my land for the purpose, I cannot claim any compensation for any diminution of value of my house caused by the noise and other inconveniences inflicted by the traffic. If, on the other hand, part of my frontage is compulsorily acquired and made part of the new highway, the position is different. Then I may claim not only the value of the land taken but also something in respect of any consequential diminution in the value of my house. In assessing this latter claim, however, regard must be had only to things done on the land taken from me.

'Where a highway is concerned, this restriction is of course artificial. The noise of traffic will begin well before it reaches the plot of land which was formerly part of my frontage and it may continue long after traffic has passed it. All the noise will contribute to any diminution of the value of my house; and it will be very difficult at times to say how much of that diminution of value is due to what the traffic does simply on the land taken from me.

F   81

'It has, however, been done by agreement in this case and the diminution in value is agreed to be £1,600. If one could take into account the total noise and inconvenience of traffic as it approached and passed the claimant's house, the compensation due to him would be £4,000 for that is the agreed total diminution in value of his house. But one cannot take such total noise and inconvenience into account for this purpose. To do so would be contrary to the true construction of the statute.'[8]

footpaths and bridleways

A footpath is defined by the National Parks and Access to the Countryside Act 1949 as 'a highway over which the public has a right of way on foot only'. A bridleway is defined by the same Act as 'a highway over which the public has the following, but no other, rights of way, that is to say a right of way on foot and a right of way on horseback or leading a horse with or without a right to drive animals of any description along the highway'. Under the Countryside Act 1968, pedal bicycles may be ridden on bridleways, but bicyclists must give way to pedestrians and persons on horseback.[9]

Some landowners put up notices saying that it is forbidden to use a pushchair or a perambulator on a public path. Though there has been no court decision on the point, such a notice is probably justified.

public path creation agreements and orders

A county council has power to make an agreement with a landowner for the dedication by the landowner of a public path or bridleway over his land. This power may be exercised by a rural district council with the consent of the county council. Public path creation agreements may provide for payment to be made to the landowner. They may also provide that the public right of way is to be limited or subject to conditions.

A county council, and a rural district council with the consent of the county council, may make public path creation orders when it is expedient to do so, bearing in mind the needs of agriculture and forestry. A council, before making an order, must be satisfied that there is need for a public footpath or bridleway, having regard to 'the extent to which the path or way would add to the convenience or enjoyment of a substantial section of the public, or to the convenience of persons resident in the area', and 'the effect which the creation of the path or way would have on the rights of persons interested in the land'. Public path creation orders, which may be either unconditional or subject to limitations and conditions, have to be confirmed by the Secretary of State for the Environment or the Secretary of State for Wales.[10] Landowners and farmers who suffer loss as a result of public path creation orders are entitled to compensation.

Where a new path or way comes into existence as a result of an agreement or order, the highway authority must carry out a survey to find out what work if any needs to be done 'to bring it into a fit condition for use by the public as a footpath or bridleway'. The authority must then carry out the necessary work.

A parish council may also make an agreement with a landowner for the dedication of a public path or bridleway over land in the parish or an adjoining parish. The council must be satisfied that an agreement would be beneficial to the inhabitants of the parish or of part of the parish. Councils have power to carry out work to maintain or improve a path so dedicated and to make arrangements with other parish councils for sharing expenses.[11]

rights of way by long use

When considering whether a footpath or bridleway has become public under the twenty-year rule, a court must look at 'any map, plan, or history of the locality or other relevant document which is tendered in evidence'.[12] In the case of *Attorney General v Meyrick and Jones*[13] an ordnance survey map of 1841 was admitted as evidence of what physical features were or were not seen by the surveyors at that date.

The case of *Jones v Bates*[14] shows how important oral evidence may be when a right of way is in dispute. Bates had used a footpath through a farm at Beckley in Sussex. Miss Jones, who owned the farm, sued him for trespass. Bates defended the case on the ground that the path was public. The county court judge decided in favour of Miss Jones, and Bates appealed to the Court of Appeal.

He called a number of people to give evidence for him. Mr Foster, who had been a tenant of the farm from 1917-34, said that in his time the path was used by many people whom he did not know. Tradespeople used it as a short cut, and sometimes people on a summer's evening would take a walk there. He said that he would not have allowed the path to be used if he had thought that he could prevent it. A Mr Reeve who had lived at the farm from 1911-16 said that strangers used the path, and that people living nearby took their Sunday evening walks there. He did not stop them because he always understood it was a public right of way. A Mr Denis, who had lived at Beckley until 1924, said that his parents had told him it was a public path, had often used it himself and had seen strangers use it many times. The path had been gravelled to make it fit for winter use, and stiles had been put up at one end. Thomas Paine had been the postman in that part of Beckley for thirty-nine years. He said that he used the footpath even when he was not delivering letters at the farm and sometimes pushed his bicycle along it.

The judges of the Court of Appeal decided that the county court judge had not given sufficient weight to the evidence. They ordered that the case should be sent back to the county court for a fresh trial.

A landowner has only himself to blame if through long use a path across his land becomes public against his wishes. Private paths and roads can be prevented from becoming public by barring them, say, once a year, or by charging a small toll occasionally. Alternatively, the landowner may put up a conspicuous notice saying that 'this is not a public path'. If the notice is torn down or defaced, he can send a written notice to the county council and the rural district council. This has the same effect as a notice beside the path.

A landowner may instead or in addition deposit with the county council and the rural district council a map of the land on a scale of not less than six inches to one mile, and a statement indicating what ways (if any) over that land he admits to have been dedicated as highways. The statement should be brought up to date every six years. Provided that this is done, the landowner can prevent any fresh rights of way from coming into being.[15]

closing a public path

County councils, and rural district councils with the consent of the appropriate county council, have power to close footpaths and bridleways. A local authority, before it exercises this power, must be satisfied 'that the path or way is not needed for public use'. Public path extinguishment orders must be confirmed by the Secretary of State for the Environment or the Secretary of State for Wales.[16]

Before confirming an order, the Secretary of State must be satisfied that the path is not greatly used by the public, and that the closure will not have a serious effect on any land served by the path. Owners and occupiers of land who suffer loss as a result of closure are entitled to be compensated. Ordinary walkers and riders, however, are not entitled to any compensation.[17]

diverting a public path

When an owner or occupier of land satisfies his local authority that his land could be used more efficiently, or a shorter route could be provided, if the path were diverted, the authority may make a public path diversion order. Orders may divert paths on to the property of other landowners. When a path leads to some place other than a road, the termination point must not be altered. When it leads to a road, the termination point may be changed, but only if the new point is not 'substantially less' convenient to the public than the old one was.

Orders must be confirmed by the Secretary of State for the Environment or the Secretary of State for Wales.[18] The Secretary of State must be satisfied that neither the public who use a path nor landowners will be seriously affected by diversion. Where a path is diverted to the property of another landowner, he will probably be entitled to compensation.[19]

maps of footpaths and bridleways

Until a few years ago, it was often very difficult to discover whether a right of way existed. Under the National Parks and Access to the Countryside Act 1949, however, county councils were required to carry out surveys of rights of way. After the surveys had been completed, the councils produced first draft maps, then provisional maps, and finally definitive maps. There was an opportunity for objection at each stage. The definitive maps which must be on view at council offices are conclusive evidence that the footpaths shown on them are public. Councils have a duty to review particulars in maps at regular intervals of not more than five years. After each review, fresh maps must be prepared.

The definitive maps were used to prepare the current series of ordnance survey maps. Broken red lines indicate bridle tracks. Lines of red dots show public footpaths. Where there is a public path over a private road or drive, it is indicated by a red 'w'.[20]

signposts

Under the Countryside Act 1968, highway authorities must put up and maintain signposts at the start of every right of way. Authorities are only exempted from this duty if the parish council or the chairman of a parish meeting, in a particular case thinks that a signpost is unnecessary. A signpost should indicate that the path is public, and if the path is well used, it should also show where the path leads and the distance or distances. Signposts must also be erected and maintained, where necessary, along the path to prevent strangers from getting lost. Persons removing or defacing signposts may be prosecuted.

Highway authorities are required to 'consult with' the owners or occupiers of the land concerned before signposting is begun. The form which consultation is to take is not specified. If an owner or occupier of land wishes to put up his own signposts without waiting for the highway authority to do so, he should ask the highway authority for consent, which no doubt is normally granted. There is however, no provision in the Act for the reimbursement of expenses.[21]

maintenance of footpaths and bridleways

Highway authorities have a duty to keep certain public paths passable and not overgrown. These are public paths created on or after 1 January 1960 under public path creation orders, public path diversion orders, and public path creation agreements.

Private persons may have an obligation to maintain certain other paths. The obligation may arise, for example, under an old enclosure order, or under a long-established custom. The existence of such an obligation may be very difficult to prove. Parish councils have, therefore, been given power to maintain any footpath or bridleway within their parishes. If the footpath or bridleway is one which the highway authority is under a duty to maintain, the authority may reimburse the whole or part of the cost.[22]

Where gates and stiles are not maintained by the highway authority or the parish council, the landowner must do the maintenance himself. He is required to keep them 'in a safe condition, and to the standard of repair required to prevent unreasonable interference with the rights of persons using the footway or bridleway.' The highway authority must contribute a quarter of the expense incurred by the landowner, and is empowered to contribute more if it wishes. There are sanctions if the landowner fails to perform his duty: the authority can, after giving fourteen days' notice, do the work itself, and can then recover the whole of the cost from the landowner without being obliged to make any contribution at all.[23]

obstructing paths

It is an offence to block a public right of way even by putting up a stile or gate, except with the consent of the highway authority. It is also an offence to put up a notice which suggests that a public path is private. A person who knows the exact route of a public path is entitled to use it, probably even though he has to trample down growing crops or cut through barbed wire. He must not, however, do more damage than is absolutely necessary. Highway authorities have the power to order landowners to lop trees where they are obstructing a path.[24]

ploughing over footpaths

If a farmer wishes to plough over a path, he should give a 'notice of intention' to the highway authority. He must make good the surface again within six weeks of the notice or within three weeks of the ploughing if he failed to give a notice. The highway authority has the power temporarily to divert a path and to grant an extension of time for making good, up to three months from the ploughing. The highway authority must take into account the interests of the users of the path. If the farmer defaults in making good, the highway authority may prosecute him, and after giving him notice itself do the work at his expense.[25]

long-distance paths

The Countryside Commission makes arrangements for the opening of long-distance footpaths and bridleways. A long-distance path does not have to be of any particular length; but it must be suitable for 'extensive journeys' on foot, horseback or bicycle. At an early stage in the planning of a route, the commission must consult all the county and district councils likely to be affected. After the consultations have been completed, the commission prepares a report containing a map of the proposed route.

The report shows what rights of way on the route exist already, and what new rights of way need to be acquired. If the route crosses a river at a point where there is no bridge the report must consider whether a ferry is needed. If more hotel or hostel accommodation is required for people using the new route, the report must recommend how it is to be provided. Attention must be given to the problem of ensuring that the new route continues to be passable. Public roads may be used for some portions of the route, and some restriction of traffic may be recommended. The report must give an estimate of the cost of the scheme.

The report is presented to the Secretary of State for the Environment or the Secretary of State for Wales.[26] The Secretary of State may accept or reject it, but he must not reject it without having discussions with the commission and with the local authorities concerned.

The commission may at any time make proposals that an established route should be varied. No variation however can take place without the approval of the Secretary of State.

Highway authorities have power to create new rights of way, and to acquire land compulsorily for hotels, hostels and restaurants.[27]

private rights of way

A person may acquire a private right of way over the land of another person; if he is the former owner he may reserve the right when he sells the land, and otherwise he may get it by express grant or by long use. If a path, a drive, or a private road is used uninterruptedly and without permission for twenty years, the owner of the land loses his right to prevent the use.[28]

The danger of not taking action to stop a trespass was

illustrated by the case of *Healey v Hawkins*.[29] Healey built a bungalow on a plot of land in the country near Rochester in 1933. He made a concrete drive along the edge of the plot which led to his garage. A Mr Cunningham was living in a small wooden bungalow next door, Cunningham's only access to the road being by a rough path. In 1938 Cunningham bought a car, and put up a garage. His own path was not wide enough or smooth enough for the car, but it was possible to reach his garage, as well as Healey's garage, by Healey's concrete drive. Cunningham did not bother to ask Healey for permission to use this but simply did so; and Healey did no more than mutter about the discourtesy. Cunningham continued to use the drive until he died, and after that, his son did so. Then some tenants took over the property, and they also used the drive, nobody troubling to ask Healey for permission.

In 1966, Hawkins succeeded the tenants. He pulled down the old wooden bungalow, and started to put up a new one. The building operations caused great inconvenience to Healey, and instead of making a proper drive of his own, Hawkins told the builders to use Healey's drive. Their lorries did so constantly, and eventually Healey lost patience and told Hawkins to stop the nuisance. Hawkins did nothing, so Healey took legal proceedings, asking the court to make an injunction against Hawkins to stop him from trespassing on the drive. The court refused. The judge said that the case was covered by the Prescription Act: nobody had asked for permission to use the drive, but it had nevertheless been used uninterruptedly by Hawkins and his predecessors for more than the twenty years required by the Act.

A landowner can, however, prevent a right of way from being used excessively, as the case of *Jelbert v Davis*[30] showed. Jelbert had bought some farmland forming part of an estate at Kenegie in Cornwall in 1961. The conveyance of the land to him said that he had the use of a right of way to it 'at all times and for all purposes.' Later, Davis and a Mr Osborne bought other portions of the estate. So long as Jelbert was farming his land, there was no trouble. In June 1966, however, the Cornwall County Council granted him permission to use the land as a caravan and camping site for not more than 200 caravans or tents from 1 April to 31 October in each year.

The right of way was a drive bordered by trees, its approach being through stone gateposts with only ten feet between them. Davis had a lodge and Osborne had a cottage just off the drive, and used the drive to bring farm carts and wagons to their land. It was obvious to them that the caravans would cause chaos. If there were 200 caravans on the site, there might be 600 people, or more, using the drive. People might go out two or three times a day in their cars, to the beach in the morning, for an outing in the afternoon, and perhaps for a drink in the evening. There would probably be serious congestion at the entrance to the drive, which was on the narrow main road between Penzance and St Ives, and there would be long delays in getting the farm vehicles in and out.

Eventually Davis and Osborne put up notices saying 'Private drive: no entry for campers or caravans.' Jelbert objected and applied to the court for a declaration that his right included a right of way for caravans and campers. Davis and Osborne counterclaimed for an injunction to prevent Jelbert from using the right of way for 200 caravans. The court decided that the use of the drive by the caravans could not be stopped but ought to be limited. Lord Denning said: 'The change from agricultural to camping land cannot be objected to, since the right covers all purposes at all times. But that is a different question from excessive user. As I read the cases there is no doubt at all that Mr Jelbert has no right under the grant to use the way to an excessive extent beyond anything that could have been within the reasonable contemplation of the parties at the time of the grant. The court cannot give any real guidance on how much user is permissible. Two hundred units is too much. We must leave it to the parties to work out what is a reasonable user.'

gates and cattle grids

In the normal way, it is unlawful to put up a gate across a road where none existed before. Landowners, however, have a right to maintain and renew gates which existed or which are presumed to have existed before a road became public.

Highway authorities may provide cattle grids to stop cattle from straying along a road. Where a cattle grid is provided, a bypass must also be provided for traffic which cannot use it, and landowners may then be compelled to take down gates. Cattle grids are usually maintained by highway authorities.[31]

closure of branch railways and country stations

The closure of branch railway lines and of country stations on main lines has caused considerable hardship to some people living in the country.

When the British Railways Board wishes to close a railway line or railway stations, it must follow the procedure which is laid down in the Transport Act 1962, amended by the Transport Act 1968. It must follow the procedure precisely, and if it does not do so, the court will intervene. This is a very important safeguard, as the case of *Warwickshire County Council v British Railways Board*[32] showed.

The Act of 1962 says that not less than six weeks before the proposed closure a notice must be published in two successive weeks in two local newspapers. The notice must also be published 'in such manner as appears to the Railways Board appropriate.' In practice this means that notices are put up at the stations affected and at nearby and terminal stations. The notice must give the date and particulars of the closure, and particulars of alternative services which are, or will be, available. It must also state that objections may be lodged with the area transport users' consultative committee within six weeks of the date given in the notice. A copy of the notice must be sent to the area committee.

Objection may be made by 'any user of any service affected' and by 'any body representing such users.' When an objection has been made, the closure must not take place until the area committee has reported to the Secretary of State for the Environment, and the Secretary of State has given his consent.

The area committee has to consider all the objections, and it must also give the Railways Board an opportunity to reply to the objections. Having done this it must prepare its report. It must draw the attention of the Secretary of State to hardship which would be caused by the closure, and it may if it wishes put forward proposals for alleviating the hardship. Having studied the report, the Secretary of State decides whether or not he will consent to the closure. Under the Act of 1968, he must have regard to social and economic considerations. If he consents, he may make the consent subject to any conditions which he thinks fit, including the provision of alternative bus services.[33]

In 1968 the Railways Board published notices saying that it wished to close the north Warwick line which ran from Stratford-upon-Avon to Birmingham by way of Henley-in-Arden. The line was useful to many people who lived in some of the more rural districts in Warwickshire and worked in Birmingham. There was a spate of objections, including one by the Warwickshire County Council. Having considered the objections, the area committee reported to the Minister of Transport that closure would cause severe hardship to a considerable number of railway passengers, especially daily travellers to Birmingham.

In spite of that report, the minister consented to the closure, but he made his consent subject to conditions. One of the conditions was that the closure should not take place until adequate additional bus services for the former rail passengers had been licensed under the Road Traffic Acts. In effect this gave the objectors another chance. They could appeal against a decision to grant road-service licences for the additional buses.

The Midland Red bus company applied to the Traffic Commissioners for licences, and the commissioners decided to grant the application. At the beginning of April 1969, the objectors appealed against the grant of licences on the ground that the proposed additional services were not adequate. They were, they said, more costly, and slower, and did not run close enough to the rail route. Long before the appeal could be heard, however, the British Railways Board published a notice saying that the line would be closed on 5 May 1969. The objectors, led by the Warwickshire County Council, applied to the court for an injunction to stop the Railways

Board from closing the line before the appeal was heard. The application for the injunction was heard by the Court of Appeal of 2 May 1969, just in time.

Dealing with the case for the Railways Board, Lord Justice Denning said that if the line were closed 'the appeal would be frustrated. The additional bus services would be on the road and the railway line would be closed, all before the appeal was heard. The board says that if the appeal was successful it would re-open the line and restore the position as it was before.

'But that is obviously no way out. By that time the passengers will all have made other arrangements for transport. Once the line is closed, the prior position cannot be restored . . . It comes then to this. The minister only gave his consent to the closure of the line of the condition that the road services licences were granted for an additional bus service. These licences have not been granted – finally granted – because they are subject to appeal and the appeal has not yet been heard. So the condition has not been fulfilled. The minister has not given his consent within . . . the Act of 1962. The closure cannot take place. I think an injunction should go to restrain them from closing the line accordingly.' The injunction prevented the Railways Board from closing the line until the appeal had been heard.

Sometimes the Secretary of State considers that an unremunerative service should be retained on social or economic grounds. In that case, if the Railways Board cannot reasonably be expected to provide the service without a grant, the Secretary of State may make a grant, for not more than three years at a time.[34]

rural bus services

An operator who wishes to start a country bus service must obtain two different kinds of licence from the traffic commissioners for his traffic area. He needs a road service licence for the service, and a public service vehicle licence for each of his buses. Public service vehicle licences are usually granted, unless the applicant is thought to be an unsuitable person, but road service licences are more difficult to obtain.

The applicant has to tell the commissioners what kind of vehicles he intends to operate, and submit proposed time-tables and faretables. The commissioners have a duty to assist a small operator adequately to present all the facts relevant to his application. The commissioners must advertise the fact that an application has been made. County and local councils, and other operators in the area, have a right to make representations and objections.

In exercising their discretion whether or not to grant a road service licence, the traffic commissioners must satisfy themselves that the proposed route is in the public interest. They must give special consideration to the needs of rural areas where bus services do not exist, or are inadequate. If the proposed service is to pass near a railway station, they must ensure that, as far as practicable, it connects with trains.

If the traffic commissioners do decide to grant a road service licence, they may attach to it such conditions as they think fit. In particular, they may require the charging of fares other than those proposed by the applicant. These may be higher than the proposed fares, if they think that the applicant is attempting to compete unfairly with established operators.

Where the applicant intends to operate minibuses carrying not more than twelve passengers, however, the traffic commissioners may dispense with this rather elaborate procedure. Provided the applicant satisfies them that there are no other transport facilities to meet the reasonable needs of people living near the proposed route, or for tourists likely to use it, they may give him a permit to run the service, instead of a road service licence. Both licences and permits have to be renewed periodically.[35]

County councils, county borough councils and rural district councils have power under the Transport Act 1968 to make grants or loans to the operator of bus services. Grants are made to assist operators 'to provide improve or continue a bus or ferry service, if in the opinion of the council, the service will be of assistance to persons living in rural areas.' The Secretary of State for the Environment may reimburse up to half the cost of making the grant or loan.[36]

canals

The owners of canals are generally bound to keep them properly dredged and fit for navigation. However, when a canal is disused and has become blocked, the courts will not force the owners to reopen it if the cost would be prohibitive.

The canals owned by the British Waterways Board are divided into three classes, the commercial waterways, the cruising or recreational waterways, and the remainder. The board has a duty to maintain the commercial waterways in a suitable condition for commercial vessels and to maintain the cruising waterways in a suitable condition for cruising craft. The performance of this duty may be enforced by the courts.

The board has power to close waterways of the third class. Privately owned canals, however, may be abandoned only by warrant of the Secretary of State for the Environment. The owners may apply for a warrant on the ground that the canal is unnecessary for the purpose of public navigation. Local authorities, and three or more owners of land adjoining a canal may apply on the ground that the canal or part of it is derelict. The Secretary of State may make it a condition of granting a warrant that the canal or part of it is transferred to a local authority or any other body. After the warrant has been granted, the Secretary of State may make an order releasing the owner from all liability to maintain the canal.

An Inland Waterways Amenity Advisory Council has been established. The duty of the council is to advise on any proposal to add to or reduce cruising waterways. It may also make recommendations for the development of canals for recreational purposes, including fishing.[37]

Scotland

In the case of a new housing development, the developer normally constructs the roads to the standard required by the local authority. When the development is complete, on the application of all the house owners, the highway authority assumes responsibility for maintenance and upkeep.

The highway authorities in Scotland are the town councils and the county councils.

Northern Ireland

Road authorities are responsible for the construction and maintenance of ordinary roads. The Ministry of Development is responsible for the construction and maintenance of trunk roads and motorways.

There is no special legislation on footpaths and bridleways, and there are no long-distance paths.

The Ministry of Development has power to subsidise unremunerative railway and bus services. The ministry also has power to authorise the abandonment of canals.

Notes to this chapter are on pages 188-9.

7 The Ownership of Land

A person may become the owner of land not by buying it, or inheriting it, but simply by long possession. Under the Limitation Act 1939, possession of land for twelve years or more may lead to ownership. The condition is that the possession must be 'adverse' to an owner of right mind and of full age. If the owner is 'under disability' the period is extended.[1]

long possession

Adverse possession means possession inconsistent with the title of the true owner. When a trespasser or a squatter remains on land without permission he takes 'adverse possession' of it. When a tenant fails to pay his rent and remains on the property, he also takes 'adverse possession'. The general rule is that if twelve years or thirty years in the case of Crown land go by, without either the owner asserting his rights or the possessor acknowledging them, the possessor becomes the owner, and may do with the property any thing which the law permits an owner to do.

Two fairly recent cases in the courts show how easily a landowner can lose all right to his property, and how essential it is for him to take action in time. The Limitation Act has nothing to do with merits.

In the first case, *Moses v Lovegrove,*[2] Mrs Moses had bought a house in 1934 at West Wickham, in Kent. At the time she bought the house it was let at a very small controlled rent to a Mr Lovegrove. He paid his rent until 1938, and then stopped. Mrs Moses took no action, perhaps because the rent was hardly worth collecting. By 1952 the house had increased in value considerably and Mrs Moses wanted possession. She sent a notice to Lovegrove putting an end to his tenancy. Lovegrove refused to move and Mrs Moses brought an action for possession in the Bromley County Court. Lovegrove contested the action on the ground that as more than twelve years had elapsed since he had last paid rent to Mrs Moses he had become the owner of the property. The judge said that Lovegrove was right. Mrs Moses appealed to the Court of Appeal and lost.

Lord Evershed said 'I think there was here undoubtedly the accrual of a right of action in May or June 1938 . . . There was then adverse possession on the part of the tenant, the defendant, until the proceedings in the present case were initiated . . . I would dismiss the appeal.'

The second case was *Hayward v Chaloner*.[3] Just before the second world war, the owner of a smallholding called Redcote Farm at Bilsthorpe in Nottinghamshire let a small part of his land to the Rector of Bilsthorpe for a nominal rent of ten shillings a year. The land was used as a garden by the tenants of a cottage belonging to the rectory.

In 1941, a Miss Stocks bought Redcote Farm. After a year or two the rector of the time ceased to pay the rent; Miss Stocks did not demand it because, as she said in evidence, 'it was the church'. In 1955, Miss Stocks sold the farm to her niece Mrs Hayward and her husband, who were prominent supporters of the church. Mr Hayward said in evidence 'I would not ask the church for ten shillings a year. If the rector had given me ten shillings I would have put it in the offertory box.' In 1962, a new rector was inducted at Bilsthorpe, the Rev Stephen Chaloner. Shortly afterwards, Mr Chaloner let the cottage to a Mr Rowlands, the proprietor of a motor-coach business. Rowlands put up a large and unsightly nissen hut in the garden and covered the ground with red shale so that he could keep motor coaches on it. Rowlands then offered to buy the cottage, and with the approval of the parochial church council, Mr Chaloner agreed to sell it. Mr and Mrs Hayward were distressed to see part of their farm being sold as a coach park, and demanded possession of the land. The rector refused to give possession. Mr and Mrs Hayward applied for possession to the Mansfield County

Court, and were given it, but the rector appealed.

In the Court of Appeal, the judges decided very reluctantly that the rector had become the owner of the land, and was entitled to sell it to Rowlands. Lord Justice Davis said that 'the plaintiffs and their aunt before them, all people, it would appear, of small means, had for many years, well over the statutory twelve years, forborne to demand the rent of ten shillings a year, and the reason for their forbearance was their loyalty and generosity to the church . . . Most unfortunately the law . . . as applied to the facts of this case, is clear and has resulted in the extinction of the plaintiffs' title to this little piece of land and its acquisition by the incumbent of Bilsthorpe.'

Lord Justice Russell added 'The generous indulgence of the plaintiffs and their predecessors in title, loyal churchmen all, having resulted in a free accretion at their expense to the lands of their church, their reward may be in the next world. But in this jurisdiction we can only qualify them for that reward by allowing the appeal and dismissing the action.'

buying land in the country

In view of the strict planning controls, there are many possible pitfalls in buying land or a house in the country, especially a building which needs to be converted. The importance of making detailed enquiries at an early stage, and not relying on statements made by the seller was well illustrated in the case of *Lake v Bushby*.[4]

Bushby owned some land near Pollington in the West Riding of Yorkshire. The land was requisitioned by the Air Ministry during the second world war, and the ministry put up some buildings including a brick hut to house airmen. When the war was over, the land was returned to Bushby and he took the buildings instead of compensation. He signed a document which stated 'It is understood that the Air Ministry can give no guarantee that the buildings comply with the bylaws, or planning requirements of the local government authorities.' The water and electricity supplies were cut off when the Air Ministry gave possession. The drains were unsatisfactory because they simply emptied into a field.

In 1946 Bushby offered the property for sale through an estate agent. The agent produced particulars which said of the hut that it 'stands on one acre of land and has water, electricity, and main drainage laid on.' Lake, having seen the particulars, inspected the property and told Bushby that he 'was looking for a place to live in with his wife. He had no money and he would have to sell his own house at Bexhill to put down the necessary purchase price.' Bushby told Lake that 'hot and cold water, electricity and drainage, would be laid on by the various undertakings.' This statement was wholly untrue.

Lake went to some solicitors in Harrogate and they agreed to act on his behalf. They took the usual step of addressing enquiries about the property to the local authority, Goole Rural District Council. In his reply, the clerk of the council wrote than 'no plans have been approved by the council for the hut referred to in your requisition.' Unfortunately, the solicitors failed to pass on the information to Lake, who sold his house at Bexhill and completed the purchase of the property at Pollington.

Shortly afterwards, Lake submitted to the Goole Rural District Council plans for the conversion of the hut to a bungalow. He also asked the electricity and water undertakings to connect supplies. The undertakings would not agree to do so, and the council refused to give planning permission for the conversion. Its main ground for doing so was that there was no water or electricity and no means for disposing of sewage. It said that the hut might have to be demolished after a year or so.

Lake, in view of the refusal of planning permission, had paid much more for the property than it was worth. He was forced to spend money in accommodating his family in a hotel after he had sold his house at Bexhill. He sued Bushby for damages for fraudulent misrepresentation and the solicitors for damages for negligence, won his case against both, and received full compensation in money. He did not, however, get the house which he had hoped to have.

rights of ownership

In 1870 a judge said that the owner of land is presumed to own everything 'up to the sky and down to the centre of the earth.' Since that time the rights of an owner have been greatly curtailed.

His ownership of the sky has been restricted by the Civil Aviation Act 1949, and the legislation which it replaced. There are restrictions also on his ownership of the soil beneath the surface of the land. He does not for example own any gold or silver contained in rocks on or under his land. He has no right to 'treasure trove'. This means gold and silver, whether in bullion, coin or some other manufactured object hidden on the land deliberately and whose true owner cannot be found. Gold and silver in mineral form and 'treasure trove' both belong to the crown.

His rights of ownership have been cut down in other ways. The Town and Country Planning Acts, the Compulsory Purchase Acts, and the Rent Acts, three examples out of many, have all restricted the right of an owner to do as he pleases with his property.

boundaries

The deeds, or the land certificate in the case of registered land, usually describe the boundaries of property in words and refer to a plan which is for the purpose of identification only. In the country, where in the past a foot or two did not matter, inspection of the property is often essential to discover the exact boundaries. If inspection is inconclusive, the ownership of a boundary hedge, wall or fence may be found by making enquiries amongst local people as to who has paid for repairs and maintenance in the past. If such a person can be found, he and his successors are presumed to be the owners.

If inspection and local enquiries fail there are certain presumptions of law regarding ownership. A boundary wall is presumed to belong equally to the owners of the land on each side. A fence is presumed to belong to the person on whose land the stakes are. When two plots of land are separated by a hedge and a ditch, there is a presumption that the hedge and the ditch belong to the owner of the land on the side of the ditch on which the hedge is. As a judge once said 'When a man digs a ditch at the limit of his land, he digs on his own land and also throws the soil excavated on to his own land.' To throw it on the land of his neighbour would be trespass. The hedge is usually planted at the top of the bank of soil which has been excavated from the ditch.

The importance of making local enquiries about boundaries is well shown by the case of *Davey v Harrow Corporation.*[5] In 1937, some builders had bought a field at Pinner in Middlesex. They proceeded to build an estate on the field, and in 1938, they sold a house on a plot at the south corner of the field to Davey. The boundary of the plot was a concrete post-and-wire fence which had been put up by the builders as close as possible to the north side of a hedge which bounded the field on the south. The hedge stood on a low bank, on the south side of which was a ditch. Beyond the ditch, was a field owned by the Harrow Urban District Council, the predecessors of the Harrow Corporation.

A number of elm trees grew on the bank, some of which were within a few feet of the fence. About 1949, cracks appeared in the walls of the house and they were found to have been caused by the taking of water by the roots of the trees from under the foundations of the house. Davey claimed compensation from the corporation. One of the questions at issue was the ownership of the trees. If Davey owned them, he was clearly not entitled to be compensated by the corporation.

In the Queen's Bench Division, the judge decided that the presumption regarding a hedge and ditch applied to the boundary between the two properties. This meant that the trees belonged to Davey. Davey appealed against this decision, and brought some fresh evidence to the attention of the Court of Appeal. In court, a member of the firm of builders said that in 1937 there had been a meeting on the site between the foreman in charge of the work and a representative of the Harrow Urban District Council. At the meeting, the council had claimed that the hedge belonged to it. The foreman had said that he had no objection, but would like to put the fence as close as possible to the hedge on its north side without destroying it. Both sides agreed that this should be done. Afterwards the council and the corporation had treated the hedge as theirs. They had cut and trimmed the grass and at some time had lopped the trees.

Lord Goddard said 'I find that whatever the true position might have been before the meeting, thereafter the bank and fence with the trees on it were regarded as the property of the council, and it has been in undisturbed possession of the bank ever since.' The court decided that the corporation was liable for the damage caused by its trees.

restrictive covenants

Landowners who sell a part of their land sometimes impose on the buyers covenants restricting the use of the land sold. The intention is usually to preserve the amenities of the neighbourhood. The growth of public town and country planning control has to some extent reduced the importance of private restrictive covenants. Nevertheless they do still have a part to play in the preservation of the countryside. They sometimes cover matters which are not covered by planning law at all. Even when there is an overlap, the landowner can enforce the covenant himself and he does not have to wait for the planning authority to act.

A restrictive covenant may remain enforceable by a landowner and his successors against a buyer of land and his successors for an indefinite time. When, however, the character of a neighbourhood has changed since a covenant was imposed, the courts may refuse to enforce it. Furthermore the Lands Tribunal has a discretionary power to modify or discharge restrictive covenants which have become obsolete or will become obsolete as a result of likely development.[6]

The case of *Chatsworth Estates Company v Fewell*[7] shows that the courts are ready to enforce restrictive covenants in suitable circumstances. Even when the character of an area has begun to change, they may be prepared to stop further deterioration.

The Dukes of Devonshire had a country house called

Compton Place, in Sussex. During the nineteenth century they built houses and hotels on part of their estate. The development became the modern town of Eastbourne. In 1897 the duke sold a house called Bella Vista, and imposed on the buyer a covenant which said that the buyer and his successors 'would not without the previous written consent of the vendor or the owner or owners for the time being of Compton Place or his or their agent use Bella Vista as a school or for any educational purpose or as a public house, or beer shop, or for any trade or business or otherwise than as a private dwelling house and also would not do or permit to be done any act or thing whatsoever which might be or become a nuisance annoyance or injury to any land of the vendor adjoining or near thereto or to the tenants of that land or any act or thing which might tend to deteriorate the value of that land.'

During the following thirty years, it appeared, the law report says, that numerous high-class schools, some blocks of flats, a hotel, and three boarding houses had been licenced in the area. There were also about half a dozen other boarding houses or guest houses of which the company had only recently become aware.

In 1927 a Mr Fewell bought Bella Vista, knowing of the covenant. Nevertheless he started to take paying guests. The guest house was extremely well managed and there was no advertisement inside or out to indicate that it was not used as a private dwelling house. But in 1928 the company heard that Bella Vista was being used as a guest house and immediately drew attention to the covenant. Fewell in reply pointed out that the character of the neighbourhood had changed and formally asked the company for its written consent to the new use of the house. The company refused, and shortly afterwards brought an action against Fewell asking for an injunction or damages.

Giving judgment, Mr Justice Farwell said 'the area remains mainly residential, although there are many flats, some few boarding-houses, some schools, and so on. Although the area is no longer confined to single dwelling-houses, and the covenants have been somewhat relaxed in the sense that some boarding-houses or guest houses have been permitted, and some other houses have been put to uses not strictly within the covenants, still, on the whole, and taking it broadly, the area still retains its character of being a residential area . . . It is quite impossible here to say that there has been so complete a change in the character of this neighbourhood so as to render the covenants valueless to the plaintiffs . . . The plaintiffs are bringing this action bona fide to protect their property, and it is hopeless to say that the change in the character of the neighbourhood is so complete that it would be useless for me to give them any relief . . .

'I am satisfied that while the use of Bella Vista as a guest house or boarding house may not at the moment cause any actual damage to Compton Place or its owners, there is a prospect of damage in the future if the defendant is allowed to continue to use Bella Vista in that way, because it might well lead to many other houses being so used which would undoubtedly damnify the owners of Compton Place.'

The court granted an injunction stopping the use of Bella Vista as a guest house.

rights of water

A landowner does not own the water in any river or stream which flows, or the water which percolates, through his land. His right to use river or stream water is limited to what is called 'ordinary and reasonable use', and he may have to obtain a licence from the appropriate river authority under the Water Resources Act 1963. No licence is normally required when water is taken for the domestic purposes of a household or for agricultural purposes other than spray irrigation. In other circumstances, however, a licence must be obtained.

A right to 'ordinary and reasonable use' means a right to take and use all water necessary for ordinary purposes in connection with his property, even though the river or stream is completely exhausted. Ordinary purposes include the watering of cattle, and domestic use. Ordinary and reasonable use also means use of water for extraordinary purposes in connection with the property so long as the use is reasonable and the water is restored to the stream afterwards substantially undiminished in volume and unaltered in character. Extraordinary purposes include irrigation.

The case of *Rugby Joint Water Board v Walters*[8] is a very important recent illustration of the law regarding the taking of water, in which the principles involved were examined at considerable length. The board was the water undertaking for the town of Rugby. Under a local Act of Parliament it had authority to take the whole flow of the river Avon at a place called Brownsover Mill, not far from Rugby. The demand for water in the Rugby area was increasing fast.

Walters owned Manor Farm, Clifton-upon-Dunsmore on the banks of the Avon, upstream from Brownsover Mill. He carried on a mixed farming business, partly arable and partly dairy. In 1959, he constructed a reservoir on part of his land, which was capable of holding 250,000 gallons. The reservoir took percolating water which would otherwise have found its way into the Avon, to the extent of about thirty to forty thousand gallons a day. At the time he constructed his reservoir, Walters bought equipment to enable him to pump water from the river and from the reservoir and to distribute it over his land in a fine spray. Shortly afterwards he began pumping. In 1963 he obtained a licence from the river authority on the footing that his use was already established when the Water Resources Act came into operation.

In December 1963, the solicitors to the water board wrote to Walters claiming that the use which he was making of the water went beyond that to which he was legally entitled as a riparian owner. They asked him for an assurance, that the use of water for spray irrigation would cease, and threatened proceedings if it did not cease. Walters ceased using water from the river but continued to use water from his reservoir. The water board accordingly brought proceedings. The board asked the court for two injunctions, one to stop permanently the taking of water from the river, and the other to stop the constant refilling of the reservoir.

In his defence Walters admitted taking river water and percolating water. He claimed however that he took the water in due exercise of his rights as a riparian owner. He denied that the taking was wrongful and he denied that the water board had suffered any damage from it. Both sides agreed that the water board was entitled to receive at Brownsover Mill 'the full and undiminished flow of the River Avon, save only so far as it might be legitimately diminished by permissible user by other riparian owners.' The question was whether the use by Walters was or was not permissible.

The evidence was that Walters was in the habit of using spray irrigation during a period extending from April to September each year. In wet summers, the period was somewhat shorter. He did not use water for irrigation every day. His maximum monthly consumption of water was probably not much more than 1.2 per cent of the monthly flow, and it was usually well below 1 per cent.

The traditional form of irrigation in this country, it was said, is flood irrigation. Under this system, water in large quantities is diverted on to the land to be irrigated, and then allowed to drain off by the ordinary force of gravity into a tail drain and so back into the water course from which it has come. Such a method requires much larger quantities than those required for spray irrigation, but a large part of the water so employed returns rapidly to the water course. By contrast, only a very small part of the water used for spray irrigation ever returns to the water course. The greater part disappears by evaporation from the soil into the atmosphere or through the crops growing on the land. Not more than 4 per cent ever returns.

Giving judgment, Mr Justice Buckley said that 'the uses to which riparian owners can put water from the stream flowing through, or past, their land should be regarded as under three distinct heads: first . . . ordinary or primary uses, for which water may be withdrawn without any obligation to return it to the stream; these uses are . . . confined to domestic uses of the kind to which water would have been put in a primitive society, such as washing, domestic consumption, watering cattle and so forth . . . Such uses are permissible regardless of their effect upon other riparian owners. Secondly, a riparian owner may use water from the stream for . . . extraordinary or secondary uses and these . . . must comply with three conditions: (a) the use must be connected with the riparian owner's riparian tenement; (b) the use must be reasonable; (c) the use must be such that the water used will be returned

to the stream substantially undiminished in volume and unaltered in character without unreasonable delay . . . Thirdly,
any other uses to which riparian owners may seek to put
water taken from the stream are impermissible however
slightly other riparian owners are affected, subject only to
the rule of de minimis . . .'

He went on to say that the decided cases showed that 'It is
not permissible to take water from a river and so use it on a
riparian tenement that much the greater part of it evaporates
either directly from the soil into the atmosphere or through
the medium of growing crops. Consequently, in my judgment
the defendant's spray irrigation cannot be justified if it is to
be considered as an extraordinary use.'

It had, Mr Justice Buckley said, been 'suggested that it
may be justified as an ordinary use; . . . that it could be regarded as analogous to mechanical garden watering . . . It is
true that a judge said that common sense would be shocked
by supposing that a riparian owner could not dip a watering
pot into the stream in order to water his garden, but he
obviously had not in mind operations on a scale comparable
with the defendant's operations. Common sense would indeed
be shocked by the idea of anyone taking tens of thousands of
gallons out of a stream by means of a watering pot to water
his garden. Hercules himself would have quailed before such
a labour . . . For these reasons I reach the conclusion that the
defendant is not entitled to take water from the Avon for
spray irrigation of his fields.

'I must now consider the question of the reservoir. Where
a stream has its source in a natural spring, the water from
which flows in a natural channel, that spring itself forms part
of the stream to the free flow of the waters of which all riparian
owners are entitled, so that to impound the water rising from
the spring infringes their rights . . . On the other hand a landowner may appropriate surface water flowing over his land
in no defined channel although the water is thereby prevented
from reaching a water course which it would otherwise supply
. . . and may also appropriate water percolating through his
land in no defined channel. There is no evidence that there has
ever been any spring feeding . . . the reservoir . . . Accordingly,
in my judgment, the water board cannot complain of the

defendant's collecting any of the water which flows into the reservoir and using it as he thinks fit. As a result of that, the water board appear to be entitled to an injunction to restrain the defendant from abstracting water from the river for the purpose of spray irrigation, but not to the injunction sought with regard to the reservoir.' A landowner may appropriate percolating water. He may have to obtain a licence under the Water Resources Act 1963, but provided he satisfies this requirement he may draw off all the water without regard to the claims of neighbouring owners or to the damage which may be done to them, even if his motive is purely malicious.

In the case of *Mayor of Bradford v Pickles*[9] the borough council had a waterworks at a place called Troopers Farm. There were many underground springs and streams beneath the land. Pickles owned some land higher up; the underground water percolated from his land to Troopers Farm. In 1892 he bored a hole in his property, saying that he wanted to drain his land so that he could dig for minerals, but it appeared that his main object was to prevent the water from reaching Troopers Farm. He hoped that the borough council would be prepared to buy his land at an excessive price in order to preserve its water supply. The mayor applied to the court for an injunction to stop Pickles from boring holes on his land.

In the House of Lords, Lord MacNaghten accepted that Pickles might be 'churlish, selfish, and grasping. His conduct may seem shocking to a moral philosopher'. However, his action was not unlawful, and the court would not make any injunction against him.

This decision was applied in the much more recent case of *Langbrook Properties Ltd v Surrey County Council*.[10] The property company owned three acres of land at Sunbury-on-Thames on which it was building shops and offices. The Surrey County Council was building a section of the M3 motorway. In the course of the work on the motorway, a number of excavations close to the land owned by the property company were made. In order to keep the excavations dry, water had to be pumped out, and as a result of the pumping underground water was taken from the land owned by the property company, and the buildings settled. The property company claimed damages for the loss, but the court decided that the Surrey County Council had not exceeded its rights in any way. The claim was dismissed.

tithe

A tithe was the right of a rector to receive a tenth part of the produce of the land in his parish. In some cases the rector was an individual person; in others the rectory belonged to a monastery which appointed a vicar to perform the necessary ecclesiastical duties 'vicariously' for the monastery. On the dissolution of the monasteries in the reign of Henry VIII, many rectories passed to the crown and were granted to laymen. The result was that in many cases laymen gained the right to tithe.

Originally tithe was payable by the owners of land in kind, a tenth of the corn, wool, milk, eggs and so on being handed to the rector, ecclesiastical or lay, and stored in tithe barns. Some tithe barns still survive. Gradually, however, money payments were substituted for tithes in kind.

In 1836 all tithes were abolished, and a tithe rent charge on land was introduced. In 1936, the tithe rent charge was itself abolished, and tithe owners were compensated by the issue to them of a Government stock, called tithe-redemption stock. The owners of land on which tithe was paid now pay a tithe-redemption annuity to the Board of Inland Revenue. The annuities are payable until 1996 and then cease. When land subject to tithe-redemption annuity changes hands, the annuity must be redeemed by a capital payment.

compulsory purchase

Ever since the building of the railways in the first half of the nineteenth century, there has been an increasing spate of legislation authorising Government departments, local authorities, and other public bodies to acquire land compulsorily.

When an authority wishes to acquire any land, it makes a provisional compulsory purchase order. The order is not effective unless and until it is confirmed by the appropriate minister. If there are any objectors, the minister[11] must hold a public enquiry, which is normally conducted by an inspector. If the order is confirmed, the authority serves on the owner a notice, known as a notice to treat. The owner has a right to have the amount of compensation due to him assessed, and normally he and the authority, after some bargaining, are able to agree a firm price. If, however, there is no agreement, the amount of compensation is assessed by the Lands Tribunal. After the compensation has been assessed, the authority may take possession at short notice.[12]

The measure of the compensation is the open market value of the land. This means the value of the land enhanced by the value of any planning permission which might be expected to have been granted in ordinary circumstances. When a building for which there is no open market, for example a church, is acquired the compensation to be paid is the cost of buying land and reinstating the building nearby. The principles on which compensation is assessed in the case of agricultural land acquired for building were discussed in the case of *Viscount Camrose v Basingstoke Corporation*.[13] Some years ago, it was decided to expand the town of Basingstoke in Hampshire. Many acres of agricultural land near the town were taken, some of it being owned by Viscount Camrose and the Hon Michael Berry. The corporation did not need to make a compulsory purchase order, as the landowners agreed to sell the land at the price which would have been payable if an order had been made.

An argument developed over the 233 acres which were furthest from the existing town centre. The Lands Tribunal thought that in the natural course of events these 233 acres would not have been developed for a long period. It valued the land accordingly at only £400 an acre, little more than the price of agricultural land. This contrasted with a valuation of £3,500 an acre for land closer to the town centre. The landowners objected that the price for the 233 acres was too low, claiming that planning permission for development had been granted and that this ought to have been taken into account.

Lord Denning said that the tribunal was right. It had to assume, for the purpose of assessing compensation, that

Basingstoke was going to expand naturally. 'Even though the 233 acres are assumed to have planning permission, it does not follow that there would be a demand for it. It is not planning permission by itself which increases value. It is planning permission coupled with demand. The tribunal thought that the demand for these 233 acres was so far distant as to warrant only a 'hope' of development, and valued them accordingly. I can see nothing wrong with this method of calculation.'

trespassers

Though notices often announce that 'Trespassers will be prosecuted', in most cases the threat is empty. Trespass is not a crime unless it is aggravated in some way. Trespass on certain public property like the railways, where the trespasser is a menace to himself and others, may entail prosecution under the bylaws or regulations. Causing deliberate harm whilst trespassing is a crime. Armed trespass is an offence under the Firearms Act 1968. Ordinary trespass, however, is a civil and not a criminal matter.

This does not mean that the landowner or tenant is without redress. Trespass is an infringement of a private right. Every house and landowner or tenant has a right to possession of his property undisturbed by trespassers. The remedy in law is to sue the offender for damages in a civil court. Most trespassing, in fact, is quite inadvertent. Many public footpaths, despite legislation to the contrary, are so badly signposted or so overgrown that it is almost impossible for a casual rambler to keep to them. Sometimes, also, a family may picnic on land which looks like a common but is really private property.

A landowner or tenant can bring a civil action against a casual trespasser, and it is no defence for the trespasser to say that he did not know he was trespassing. Judges, however, do not like to have their time wasted by cases where the trespasser acted innocently and did no real damage. A landowner or tenant who was ill-advised enough to sue an inadvertent trespasser would be unlikely to be awarded damages of more than a few new pence and might very well be ordered to pay

H   113

the costs of the proceedings which would certainly amount to a great deal more.

Deliberate and persistent trespass is, of course, a different thing. The landowner or tenant can apply to the court for an order, an injunction, to the offender to stop trespassing. If an injunction is disobeyed, the offender may be committed to prison for contempt of court.

There is a civil remedy for damage done by trespassers even though the damage was unintended. If growing crops have been trampled on, or fences broken, or if gates have been left open so that cattle have strayed, the owner or the tenant of the land is entitled to full compensation for the harm caused. The trespasser would almost certainly have to pay the costs of the proceedings as well as the damages to the owner.

A landowner or tenant who finds a trespasser on his land is justified in asking the trespasser to leave immediately. If the trespasser refuses, he may be ejected, but no greater force than is absolutely necessary to achieve the purpose must be used.

In the case of *Hemmings v Stoke Poges Golf Club*,[14] the Court of Appeal decided that the moderate amount of force used was justified. Hemmings had become an employee of the Stoke Poges Golf Club in Buckinghamshire in 1909. He had some duties to perform at the clubhouse in the evenings, and he lived in a tied cottage in the grounds. During the first world war, he was exempted from military service. In April 1918, however, he was required by the local military tribunal to do farm work, as a condition of this exemption. In May he left the employment of the club and went to work for a nearby farmer. The club engaged a new employee whom it wanted to live in the cottage, and gave Hemmings notice to quit in June. Hemmings, however, had not been given accommodation on the farm. He had nowhere to go, and he refused to leave.

The club asked an estate agent to evict Hemmings and his family. In August 1918 the agent went to the cottage with three or four men. Using no more force than was necessary, they pushed Hemmings and his wife and child out of the cottage, and removed the furniture to an adjoining garage.

Nobody was injured, and the furniture was not damaged. Hemmings and his wife brought an action claiming damages for assault and trespass.

In the Court of Appeal Lord Justice Scrutton said that 'this case raises a legal question of great interest and general importance. Shortly stated the question is whether if an owner of landed property finds a trespasser on his premises, he may enter the premises and turn the trespasser out, using no more force than is necessary to expel him, without having to pay damages for the force used . . . Of course he may.' The court rejected the claim.

The decision is still good law on the general issue of how to deal with a trespasser who will not leave property voluntarily. Forcible ejection of an occupier from a dwelling house however is now a criminal offence (see page 150). An occupier is a person who has been a tenant or licensee of the owner, but not a person who has always been a trespasser.[15] If a trespasser enters, or tries to enter, property forcibly, the owner is immediately entitled to use moderate force to repel him. The law assumes that the owner will not be able, by peaceful means, to persuade him to depart, and there is no need for the owner to try. If the trespasser actually assaults the owner or one of his employees, the person assaulted may use as much force as is necessary to stop the assault, even though the trespasser may suffer bodily harm as a result of the action.

It is perfectly lawful to keep guard dogs to protect property, but it is illegal to set spring guns or any kind of mantrap with the intention of killing or maiming trespassers. Landowners who keep guard dogs should put up notices to warn trespassers of the risks they are running.

A trespasser has few rights. The owner must not deliberately injure him, and must not carry out a dangerous operation on his land when he knows that there is a trespasser present who may be injured by the operation. Otherwise, the trespasser is entirely at his own risk. A trespasser who is injured by a bull, or who breaks his leg in a dangerous hole, has no grounds in law for complaint.

Young children, however, are privileged. The law recognises that they may be attracted on to land, for example because there is a pond or a lake, because there is some unusual machinery, or because there are plenty of blackberries to pick. If a landowner knows that children are in the habit of entering his property, he must take reasonable care for their safety. It is no defence for him to say that he did not invite the children to play there, or even, probably, that he always turns children out when he sees them.

The duty of care towards children, and towards trespassers in general when a dangerous operation is being carried out was well illustrated by the case of *Mourton v Poulter*.[16] Though the case involved a contractor, the principles of law apply equally to landowners.

A man called Ferris owned some open land at Acton in London on which he intended to build some houses. Children were in the practice of using the land, which was in a derelict condition and unfenced, as a playground. There was an elm tree some fifty to sixty feet high which had to be removed before the intended building work could be carried out. Ferris engaged Poulter, a nurseryman of long experience, to cut the tree down. The work began on a Friday. On the following Tuesday, it was expected that the tree would fall, and in anticipation a large number of children arrived and gathered round the tree. About noon, Poulter drove the children back from the tree, but they returned to it. Between three and four in the afternoon, his assistant again drove them back, but again they returned. About five the tree was being held up by one root only, and Poulter knew that when the root was cut, the tree would fall within about two minutes. At 5.15, Poulter or his assistant without giving any further warning to the children who were standing round, cut the root, and the tree fell. Three boys were caught by the fall of the tree. Two of the boys were not injured, but the third, Herbert Mourton who was ten years old, was crushed and injured.

The father of Herbert brought an action against Poulter for damages for personal injuries. The case was heard by the judge of the Brentford County Court. Mourton alleged that Poulter had been negligent in causing the tree to fall on Herbert, in failing to give Herbert any warning that the tree was about to fall, and in not moving Herbert to a place of safety. Poulter in reply denied that he was negligent. If he had been negligent, however, he added that he had no duty of care towards Herbert, because Herbert was a trespasser on the land where the tree had stood.

The county court judge dismissed the claim. It was true the judge said, that Poulter had been negligent in not giving a warning, and if Herbert had been invited on to the land to watch the felling, Poulter would have been liable. Herbert, however, was a trespasser, and there was no need to take care of a trespasser. Mourton appealed. The judges of the Court of Appeal reversed the decision. 'In the present case,' Lord Justice Scrutton said, 'the defendant was a man experienced in felling trees, who knew the time when the tree would probably fall, and the distance it would probably cover when it fell. He cut the last root by which the tree was supported, knowing that the tree would fall in about two minutes and that children were standing round, without giving any warning . . . In a case such as this the person who is about to do a dangerous act is under a duty to warn even trespassers. The liability of an owner of land to trespassers does not arise where there is on the land a continuing trap, such as [in an American case] an innocent-looking pond which contained poisonous water . . . There, as the land remains in the same state, a trespasser must take it as he finds it, and the owner is not bound to warn him. That, however, is a different case from the case in which a man does something which makes a change in the condition of the land, as where he starts a wheel, fells a tree, or sets off a blast when he knows that people are standing near. In each of these cases he owes a duty to these people, even though they are trespassers, to take care to give them warning . . . I am therefore of opinion that this appeal should be allowed.'

In some cases, however, the responsibility for the safety of their children rests with the parents rather than with the occupiers of the land. In the case of *Phipps v Rochester Corporation*[17] the corporation was about to build some houses on a field on the outskirts of the city. In the middle of the open space, its workmen had dug a long deep trench in order to lay a sewer. Two children, Yvonne and Ian Phipps, aged seven and five, lived in a house nearby. One evening in October 1951, Yvonne came back from school and took her brother to pick blackberries in the field. Yvonne saw the trench in time, and managed to avoid it, but Ian fell in and broke his leg.

Their father sued the corporation for damages. He said that the workmen employed by the corporation ought to have been well aware that children were in the habit of playing in the field or crossing it. Despite this, they had failed to fence or guard the trench, or to take any other steps to prevent children from falling into it. The court, however, decided that the corporation was not liable. Mr Justice Devlin said: 'I have to consider whether the corporation ought . . . to have anticipated the presence of Ian . . . unaccompanied. I say "unaccompanied" because Yvonne, while doubtless able to take care of herself as is shown by her own evidence of the trench, was not old enough to take care of her little brother as well . . . I do not think that the corporation ought to have anticipated that it was a place in which children of five would be sent out to play by themselves . . . The houses have gardens in which children can play . . . Even if it be prudent, which I do not think it is, for a parent to allow two small children out in this way on an October evening, the parents might at least have satisfied themselves that the place to which they allowed their little children to go held no danger for them . . . The corporation is entitled to assume that parents will behave in this naturally prudent way, and is not obliged to take it upon itself, in effect, to discharge parental duties.'

grants for improvement

Under the Housing Act 1969, grants for improvement are made by local authorities, that is to say the councils of boroughs, urban districts, and rural districts. The grants are of three kinds, standard grants, special grants, and improvement grants.

To qualify for a standard grant, an applicant must be the owner, or a tenant under a lease which has at least five years to run, of a property built before October 1961. The property must lack 'standard amenities': these are a supply of water, a bath, a wash basin, a lavatory and a sink.

If an owner or a tenant qualifies and intends to install 'standard amenities', he may make an application for a grant to his local authority. He should not start the work before making the application. Local authorities do, however, have a discretion to accept late applications if they are satisfied that there were good reasons for starting the work. The application must give the name of the property and must specify the work which is to be carried out. If only some of the standard amenities are to be provided, the applicant must state whether or not the remainder have already been provided.

When considering applications the local authority has to satisfy itself that on the completion of the work the property will have all the standard amenities and will be in good repair, 'having regard to its age, character, and locality'. No attention is to be paid to the decorative order of the property inside, but the local authority must be satisfied that the property is likely to remain 'fit for human habitation and available for use as a dwelling' for a substantial period, normally at least fifteen years. If the local authority is satisfied it must approve the application for the grant, and if it is not satisfied it must refuse it.

Standard grants are paid when the work is completed to the satisfaction of the local authority. The authority may require completion within a fixed period which must not, however, be less than a year.

The amount of the standard grant is half the cost, within certain limits. The normal limit at the time of writing for all the amenities is £200. This sum is made up of £75 for a bath together with the plumbing, £50 for a lavatory £45 for a sink together with the plumbing, and £30 for a washbasin together with the plumbing. Nothing is paid for a second amenity of the same description, for example a second bath or a second lavatory. The total limit is, however, raised to £450 if a supply of water has to be brought into the property for the first time, if a completely new bathroom has to be built, or if a septic tank or cesspool has to be provided.

Standard grants for houses in multiple occupation are called special grants. The maximum amount payable for each amenity is the same, but grants may be paid for second and further amenities in suitable cases. There is no overall limit of £200 or £450.

Improvement grants may be paid to owners and tenants for the improvement of their property. The leases of tenants must have at least five years to run. Improvement other than the provision of standard amenities is not defined but it includes the conversion into a house of a building such as a barn, a mill, an oast-house, or a school. Any proposed improvement which will cost £100 or more may qualify, but local authorities have an absolute discretion to reject applications or to allow less than the maximum amount so long as they give their reasons in writing.

Applications should be made before work is started, unless there are special reasons. Applications must give particulars of the proposed work and an estimate of the cost; and the local authorities must satisfy themselves that the property after improvement will provide satisfactory housing accommodation for a substantial period.

When an application is accepted, the authority determine what is a reasonable sum for the work. The maximum grant is generally half this sum up to a ceiling of £1,000, or £1,200 in the case of the conversion of a house or other building of three or more storeys. A grant may be paid either when the work has been completed or by instalments as it progresses.

The Act does not require authorities to demand the repayment of a grant if the property is sold. This is presumably a matter for each authority to decide for itself.[18]

Scotland

In Scotland, it is not possible to acquire a good title to land by long possession only. If, however, a person has lawful possession of land uninterruptedly for ten years, although his title may be defective, no one can claim that he has a faulty title.[19]

Boundaries are usually described accurately in deeds. If there is any uncertainty about boundaries, owners may for a small charge examine old deeds at the General Register of Sasines in Edinburgh. All deeds under which land in Scotland is transferred must be registered there.

Covenants affecting land run with the land when property

changes hands. Under the Conveyancing and Feudal Reform (Scotland) Act 1970, it is possible to apply to the Lands Tribunal for the modification or abolition of covenants which appear to be of an unduly restrictive nature, or which, owing to the passage of time, have ceased to be of any importance.

In Scotland the owners of land in most cases pay an annual charge called a feuduty to a person known as a superior. When land was originally sold, it used to be the practice of the seller to require the price to be paid partly in capital and partly by way of an annual charge which continued in perpetuity. In this way the original owner of land and his successors retained an interest in the land as superior and could ensure that the covenants they imposed were observed. The practice of paying feuduties to a superior is derived from the feudal system of land tenure, and moves for the abolition of this system in Scotland have been made.

Northern Ireland

There is no equivalent to the Water Resources Act 1963, and it is not, therefore, necessary to obtain a licence before taking water.

Tithe was abolished in 1838.

Notes to this chapter are on pages 189-190.

8 Neighbours

Problems involving neighbours are almost bound to arise from time to time. In the country, overhanging and dangerous trees, weeds, the right to light, excessive noise, and smells, are a common cause of dispute.

overhanging trees

Trees have no respect for walls and fences, but when branches and roots spread over and under neighbouring properties, they infringe the right of the owners to the unrestricted use of their land. The neighbours are entitled, so far as the law is concerned, to lop off the intruding part without notice, even though lopping may kill the tree. Behaviour of this kind, however, almost inevitably leads to ill-feeling, and a wise person tries to seek the co-operation of his neighbour before taking the law into his own hands. It should be borne in mind that fruit on an overhanging branch belongs to the owner of the tree.

The leading case on overhanging branches is *Lemmon v Webb*.[1] Lemmon and Webb were the owners of adjoining land. Lemmon had a large number of old trees which grew close to the boundary fence. Some of the branches overhung the fence, having done so for many years, and without warning Lemmon, Webb cut off a number of these, back to the boundary fence. Lemmon was incensed, brought proceedings against Webb and asked the court for a declaration that Webb was not entitled to cut off branches which had overhung for many years. Alternatively, he asked for a declaration that Webb was not entitled to act without giving due notice. He

122

also claimed an injunction to stop Webb from any further cutting or lopping, and damages for trespass and wrongful cutting.

In the Chancery Division of the High Court, Mr Justice Kekewich said that: 'a neighbour's tree overhanging my land . . . is a nuisance of omission, that is to say it is negligence on the part of the owner of the tree to allow the branches to overhang the land . . . The person suffering the nuisance is entitled to abate it, but on giving notice. Of course, that means reasonable notice, the object . . . being that the owner of the tree should have a fair opportunity of abating the nuisance while preserving his own property . . . In this case the opportunity was not given, and there really is no justification for not giving it . . . I do not think that there is any occasion for a declaration, and the justice of the case will be met by asking the defendant to pay £5 damages, and the costs of the action in the High Court.'

Webb appealed, and won. Lord Justice Lindley's comment in the Court of Appeal was: 'the law on the subject is, in my opinion, as follows. The owner of a tree has no right to prevent a person lawfully in possession of land into or over which its roots or branches have grown from cutting away so much of them as projects into or over his land, and the owner of the tree is not entitled to notice unless his land is entered in order to effect such cutting. However old the roots or branches may be, they may be cut without notice, subject to the same condition. The right of an owner or occupier of land to free it from such obstructions is not restricted by the necessity of giving notice, so long as he confines himself and his operations to his own land, including the space vertically above and below its surface.' Lord Justice Kay spoke unfavourably on the conduct of Webb. 'In my opinion, it would be better if the law were that, before cutting a neighbour's trees, notice should be given in order to afford to the owner of the trees an opportunity of removing the boughs which occasion a nuisance . . . No one but an ill-disposed person would do such an act without previous notice. There was no emergency in this case. The defendant has acted in an unneighbourly manner and I cannot help thinking that he intended to cause annoyance. I do not think he ought to have any costs of the action, and I was reluctant to give him costs of the appeal.'

Despite the unfavourable comments of the judges, the law remains the same now as it was in 1894. No notice is necessary unless the land of the owner of the tree is entered.

A landowner must ensure that his trees do not cause damage to the properties of his neighbours. The case of *Davey v Harrow Corporation*[2] has already been mentioned on page 103. Another important case is *McCombe v Read*.[3]

In the early years of the twentieth century, Enfield in Middlesex, was still rural, and a property called Highfield House stood almost isolated, in open country. In 1911, however, another house, Wissenden, was built close to its boundary fence, and the owner of Highfield House wishing to screen his property from Wissenden, planted a row of lombardy poplars between six and eight feet from the fence.

McCombe bought Wissenden in 1944, when it was apparently still in a sound condition. A few years later, however, cracks began to appear in the walls. McCombe had some experience of damage caused to buildings by the roots of poplars, and suspected that the roots of the trees in the grounds of Highfield House were the cause of the trouble. He spoke to Read, the owner of Highfield House, asking him to inspect the damage, and to cut down the poplar trees. Read did nothing. McCombe brought an action claiming damages, and asking for an injunction to restrain Read from allowing the roots of trees to do damage to Wissenden.

At the hearing, a forestry expert gave evidence. He said that a poplar tree would transpire twelve thousand gallons of water in a season. Poplars, being in a row, would compete with each other and send their roots straight out before them. The houses at Enfield were built on boulder clay. When water is taken from the soil on a large scale by tree roots, the clay shrinks, and house walls crack and subside. The court, having heard the evidence, decided that McCombe was entitled to both damages and an injunction.

dangerous trees

The owner or occupier of land is liable to his neighbour

and to the public for injuries caused to them by trees on the land. He can only escape liability if he never knew nor ought to have known that the tree which caused the injury was dangerous.

In the case of *Caminer v Northern Investment Trust Ltd*,[4] the House of Lords decided that the occupier was not liable.

There were a number of elm trees standing in the forecourt of a block of flats called St. James' Close in Prince Albert Road, St John's Wood, London. The company was landlord of the block. It employed a well-known firm of estate agents to manage the property, and the estate agents in turn employed a timber contractor who had been engaged in timber felling for more than thirty years. In March 1947, the estate agents and the timber contractors decided that the elms, which were in front of the flats, should be lopped and topped. The object was to open up the gardens to light and air to enable grass and flowers to grow more freely. Nobody had the safety of the trees in mind. In any event by April 1947 only a little of the work had been carried out.

On 7 April 1947, a fine but rather gusty day, Mr and Mrs Caminer were driving along Prince Albert Road when one of the elms which had not yet been lopped fell on their car. The car was wrecked, and they were injured. They sued the company for damages, alleging negligence. The tree was found to be a large well-grown elm, between 120 and 130 years old. Three of its roots were discovered to be badly affected by a disease called elm-butt rot; the other three roots showed signs of rot, but were less badly affected. The disease was of long standing and must have been present in the roots for many years before the company had become the landlord of St James' Close. The rot, however, had not taken a normal course, inasmuch as the fungus which had caused it was working out sideways along the main roots and had not affected the trunk. There was nothing, therefore, to indicate by external examination that the tree was in any way diseased, and even if the trunk had been bored it was very unlikely that the existence of the disease would have been discovered.

The tree carried a considerable crown, some thirty-five feet across. The evidence was 'that the fall was due to a combination of circumstances, namely, the action of the wind on a tree bearing a large crown, the roots of which had rotted to a greater or less extent, and the failure to trim or lop the tree or its branches. Had it not been for the condition of the roots, it is probable that the wind would not have been heavy enough on the day in question to cause the tree to fall. On the other hand had the tree not been bearing so much top hamper, and had it been topped or pollarded, there is no reason to suppose that the tree would have fallen when it did, and it might have stood for a very long time.'

Counsel for Mr and Mrs Caminer in the House of Lords did not allege that the company were to blame for its failure to discover that the roots were diseased. He did, however, argue that 'in the particular circumstances of the case the company was under a duty as a reasonable landowner in the management of its property to lop, top or pollard this elm tree and that, if such action had been taken, the tree would not have fallen when it did, and Mr and Mrs Caminer would not have suffered the damage complained of.' He continued that it was 'well-known that an elm tree is dangerous, treacherous, and shallow-rooted; and that either the branches are or the whole tree is liable to fall suddenly; that this was a large tree and well into middle-age, situated close to a busy thoroughfare, and carried a considerable crown . . . and that for these reasons this particular tree ought to have been suspected and dealt with.'

The House of Lords however did not agree that there was any such duty to lop the tree. Giving judgment, Lord Porter said: 'I do not regard the evidence as establishing that elm trees are so plainly a danger as to require their being lopped and topped lest they should fall when to all external appearance they are sound and no inspection would raise a doubt as to their general condition. If such a duty existed there would be, I imagine, a vast number of negligent persons who are only saved from liability owing to the chance that their elm trees have in fact resisted the forces tending to make them fall.' Mr and Mrs Caminer failed to recover damages and had to pay the costs of the proceedings.

In a later case, *Quinn v Scott and the National Trust*,[5] the injured person was more fortunate. On 16 August 1961, a Mr Quinn was driving a minibus along the main A614 road from Doncaster to Nottingham, carrying workmen from a building site near Doncaster to their homes at Nottingham. Near Worksop the A614 runs by Clumber Park, which belongs to the National Trust. In Clumber Park, very close to the road, there was a belt of hardwood trees, including beeches. As Quinn was passing Clumber Park, he saw a beech tree falling across the road in front of him. He stopped his minibus quickly, and did not hit the fallen tree. A car coming the other way, however, driven by a man called Scott, was unable to stop: its windscreen was broken and the car was filled with leaves, Scott was temporarily blinded, and his car ran into the minibus.

Quinn claimed damages for negligence against both Scott and the National Trust. The court decided that Scott could not reasonably have been expected to have avoided the accident and that he was not negligent. The court then considered the question of the liability of the National Trust. The evidence was that 'the tree of which a large portion fell was one of a belt of broad-leaved trees of various species which bordered the road for a distance of about a mile and included a number of beech trees. The beech trees were about two hundred years old, that is to say, nearing the end of their normal expectation of life, but not necessarily senile . . . There had at that time been visible signs in the tree of thinness of foliage and of die-back in the crown (that is to say dead branch tips), indicating that the tree was unhealthy. These signs ought to have been noticed on the various inspections of the trees by the forester or woodmen. Either they were not noticed or, if noticed, they were not thought sufficiently significant to be reported to the land agent of the National Trust.'

Mr Justice Glyn-Jones gave judgment that 'my task in this case is to decide what is the duty resting on the National Trust, and whether or not any breach by the National Trust is established. The duty of the National Trust is to take such care as a reasonable landowner – and that means a prudent landowner – would take to prevent unnecessary danger to users of the highway adjoining the National Trust's land. There is not to be imputed in the ordinary landowner the knowledge possessed by the skilled expert in forestry . . . In my opinion, however, there may be circumstances in which it is incumbent on a landowner to call in somebody skilled in forestry to advise him, and I have no doubt but that a landowner on whose land this belt of trees stood, was under a duty to provide himself with skilled advice about the safety of the trees . . .

'The facts which were, or should have been, known to the National Trust were as follows. This tree, which was between 90 and 100 feet tall, stood 53 feet west of the carriageway of a busy main road on which much traffic moved at high speeds, and some at very high speeds. There was no protection for the tree against winds blowing from a westerly direction. If the whole tree, or part of the bole carrying one or more of the stems, fell towards the road, the carriageway would be completely blocked . . . The tree was old and had reached a stage when decay was to be apprehended . . . There was . . . the appearance of unhealthiness in the thinness of the foliage and the indications of die-back . . . If, being apprised of these facts, it were suggested to the reasonable landowner that he might postpone the felling of the tree until the next felling programme was carried out . . . I am clearly of the opinion that the reasonable landowner would say, or ought to say, "I will not take the risk . . . If [the tree] falls across the road the consequences may well be disastrous. I will not wait. Let the tree be cut down at once." '

Mr Justice Glyn-Jones decided that the National Trust had not acted as a reasonable landowner would or ought to have done, and he ordered it to pay £2,500 to Quinn. He did, however, express some sympathy for the National Trust: 'The commercial grower of timber will not normally leave a tree standing . . . after the time in its life when the risk of decay outweighs any advantage of further growth. From a purely commercial point of view, these trees would have been cut down years ago. But the good landowner – using the word "good" in its moral sense – does not ruthlessly cut down every tree growing on his land as soon as it would pay him to do so. He has some regard for the beauty of the tree and of the countryside. The National Trust is, and must be, careful to have in mind what is called the amenity value of growing trees . . . I am, however, . . . bound to take the view that in the present case the safety of the public must take precedence

128

over the preservation of the amenities, and cannot hold that the trust's duty to care for the countryside diminishes in any degree the duty not to subject users of the highway to unnecessary danger.'

weeds

A landowner is not liable to his neighbour if he allows weeds to grow and the wind to spread their seeds. This was decided in the case of *Giles v Walker*.[6] Giles and Walker farmed neighbouring land. Walker's property had been woodland until about 1885, when it was cleared. As soon as Walker began to cultivate it, thistles sprang up all over. He did nothing to prevent the thistles from seeding, and in 1887 and 1888 thousands of thistles were in full seed, the seeds being blown by the wind in large quantities on to the Giles' adjoining land, where they took root and did damage.

Giles sued Walker for damages in the county court. The county court judge decided that Walker had been negligent and awarded damages against him. Walker appealed, and, in the Court of Appeal, Lord Coleridge gave one of the shortest judgments on record. 'I never heard such an action as this' he said. 'There can be no duty as between adjoining owners to cut the thistles, which are the natural growth of the soil. The appeal must be allowed.'

Landowners have, however, some protection under the Weeds Act 1959. If the Minister of Agriculture, Fisheries and Food is satisfied that 'injurious weeds', which include thistles, dock, and ragwort, are growing on any land, he may serve a notice on the occupier. The notice requires the occupier within a definite time to take action to stop the weeds from spreading. If the occupier fails to take action, he may be prosecuted, and the work may be carried out by the ministry or the local authority at his expense.

light

The general rule is that nobody is entitled to daylight

through his windows. There is, however, a very important exception to the rule. If a landowner and his predecessors have had daylight through their windows for twenty years or more, he and his successors will have acquired a right to continue to have a reasonable amount of light through them as long as the house stands.[7] His neighbour is not entitled to put up a building which substantially interferes with his light. The technical name of this right is 'ancient lights', though there need be nothing very ancient about them. Many houses which were built after the end of the last war have now acquired 'ancient lights.'

'Ancient lights' can only prevent building. They do not protect a landowner from having his rooms darkened by a tree growing on the land of his neighbour. They do not apply to gardens. There is nothing (except the town and country planning or the local building regulations) to stop a person from putting a high wall round his garden even though it darkens a neighbouring garden. There is nothing (except the road traffic laws) to prevent the regular parking of a large lorry outside a window.

How much interference from a building is substantial? A rough rule is that if light comes to windows at an angle of 45° or less from the horizontal, there is no cause for complaint. The angle must be greater than 45° to make a substantial interference. There is, however, nothing official about this rule. In the words of one of the judges, the real test is: 'Does the interference make the light insufficient according to the ordinary notions of mankind for the comfortable use and enjoyment of the house as a dwelling house, if it is a dwelling house, or for the beneficial use and occupation of the buildings if it is a warehouse, shop, or other place of business?'

Ough v King[8] is a recent case on light. Mrs Ough bought an old house at Gravesend in Kent in 1957. She was a minister in a church known as the United Fundamentalist Church, and one of her duties was to send the literature of the sect to people all over the world. She employed a number of voluntary helpers, and she and they used a ground floor room in her house as an office.

In 1963, King, a builder, bought the house next door with

a view to converting it into self-contained flats. He was given planning permission and got on with the work. The conversion involved putting a kitchen in place of a conservatory on the ground floor, and building an extension for a bathroom on the first floor. As the building work progressed, Mrs Ough found that her ground floor room became darker, and it became more difficult to work there without using artificial light. Mrs Ough took proceedings, alleging that her right to daylight had been infringed; she asked for damages of £400 and an injunction requiring King to remove the extensions. The judge of the Gravesend County Court decided that her right had been infringed. Exercising his discretion as to the appropriate remedy, he awarded £300 damages but refused to make the injunction.

King appealed against the award of damages to the Court of Appeal. He lost his appeal. According to Lord Denning: 'It is not every diminution of light which gives a right of action. It is only when it is so diminished as to be a nuisance. It means that Mr King was not allowed to build next door in such a way as to deprive Mrs Ough of the light coming to her room as to make it uncomfortable according to the ordinary notions of mankind . . . Before the building the room was a light room. By the loss it has suffered it has become a slightly less than light room. It now receives less light than is sufficient according to the ordinary notions of mankind.'

A person who contemplates building at some time in the future can prevent a neighbour who has a fairly new house from acquiring 'ancient lights'. This is done by registering a notice with the local authority under the Rights of Light Act 1959, section 2.

noise

Everyone has a right to a reasonable amount of peace and quiet in his own home, and the courts will give protection against unreasonable disturbances caused by other people. When is a disturbance unreasonable? There are no hard and fast rules. The law gives a rough guide: the test of unreasonableness is whether objection to the conduct could be taken by a reasonable man living in the neighbourhood. The courts have said on many occasions that a reasonable man would be prepared to endure more noise and inconvenience in a poor residential area than in a good one. He would put up with greater disturbance in a town than in the country.

Another way of expressing the question is to ask whether a particular noise is natural to, and not excessive for, the area. A person living in a busy shopping street is bound to get noise from the traffic, from shoppers in the daytime, and from people looking in the lighted windows at night. In an industrial area, factory sirens and a moderate amount of noise when shift workers go on and off duty may be expected. The sound of lorries being loaded and unloaded, and perhaps the whirring of machinery are natural noises. In the country, the local sounds, such as the braying of a donkey, the crowing of a cock, and the occasional barking of a dog will be heard. People who live near farms can expect to hear some noise early in the morning.

Everyone must be prepared to put up with some inconvenience. Neighbours will probably have workmen in from time to time to do necessary repairs and maintenance work. They may have children, who are likely to be noisy sometimes.

The courts deal with each complaint on its merits. Often they refuse to make injunctions. In one case some noise from a factory, and in another case a reasonable amount of noise from a dairy, were not considered to be sufficient nuisance. A vicar was told that his congregation would have to put up with a humming noise from a nearby electricity generating station during services. People living near a church were told that it was perfectly reasonable for the bells to be rung before communion on Sunday mornings. The owners of houses near a football ground alleged that the crowds disturbed their peace by cheering and waving rattles, but the court refused to prevent matches from being played there on Saturday afternoons.

In other cases, however, the courts have thought the complaint justified, and stopped the nuisance. Factory owners have been told that their machinery was too noisy, and have been ordered to do something about it. The owners of a funfair have been instructed to close down at a reasonable time in the evenings. The owners of a dance hall have been told to have their premises sound-proofed. The proprietors of a night club have been ordered to take steps to prevent noisy crowds from gathering outside.

The cases of *Leeman v Montagu*[9] and *Goodier v Warfield Kennels Ltd*[10] throw some light on the rights of the countryman to peace and quiet. Thorpe is a village, in residential country not far from Egham in Surrey. Warfield is a village of a similar kind near Bracknell in Berkshire. Both villages have for many years been popular living places for business and professional people working in London.

Leeman bought Thorpe Cottage in September 1935. The house was next to a farm owned by a man called Montagu, who at that time was keeping about 750 cockerels in an orchard about a hundred yards away from the house. Leeman and his wife were wakened by crowing at two in the morning, and the noise continued until about eight so that they had no sleep. After a few nights Leeman complained to Montagu who said that he was selling cockerels daily and hoped to have them all sold within a month. Leeman and his wife went away for a few days, but they still found the noise unbearable when they returned. They were compelled to sleep with cotton wool in their ears and with the windows closed.

An angry correspondence ensued. Finally, Leeman gave Montagu fourteen days in which to move his cockerels. Montagu moved them just before the time-limit expired, and was warned by Leeman that action would be taken if the nuisance was repeated. There was no noise until May 1936, when Montagu put 200 cockerels into the orchard. Leeman immediately brought proceedings for an injunction to stop Montagu from using the orchard to keep cockerels.

At the hearing, a number of people gave evidence: Montagu said that he had spent a large sum of money on the farm, and that the cockerels were the most important part of his business; he could not rearrange the farm so as to move the cockerels away from the orchard. Two witnesses gave evidence for Leeman. The previous owner of Thorpe Cottage compared the noise of the cockerels to the sound of a football crowd cheering at a cup-tie. A poultry expert said that he thought Montagu could rearrange his farm without difficulty.

Four witnesses gave evidence for Montagu. The last owner

but one of Thorpe Cottage said that he had suffered no inconvenience from the noise. A man who always spent the summer
at Thorpe in a house 140 yards from the orchard said he
had never been wakened by cockerels. A nurseryman who
lived 200 yards from the orchard said that he had never been
disturbed by the cockerels, though he could hear them if he
listened. An expert said that the farm was one of the best-
arranged farms in the country.

The result of the case was, in a sense, a draw. The court
made an injunction ordering Montagu 'not to carry on his
business as a poultry breeder in such a way as to be or cause
a nuisance to Leeman and unlawfully to interfere with his
occupation and enjoyment of the cottage.' The judge added,
however, that he would not regard it as a breach of the injunction without much more definite evidence, if Montagu
were to use the far side of his orchard for keeping cockerels
in normal breeding pens.

The case of *Goodier v Warfield Kennels Ltd* was brought
by three London businessmen who lived at Warfield. They
complained that the dogs at a nearby greyhound kennels were
constantly barking at night and interfering with their sleep.
Furthermore the kennels were running an electric hare very
early in the mornings, and the noise of the machinery woke
them. The three men brought an action in the High Court to
stop the disturbance.

During the course of the hearing, the judge, Mr Justice
Hinchcliffe, decided to make an early-morning visit to Warfield to assess for himself the extent of the annoyance. This
was unusual, as judges normally rely entirely on the evidence
of the witnesses in the case.

The injunction was granted. The kennel owners were told
that the barking of their dogs and the noise caused by the
running of the electric hare had caused a serious nuisance.
They were ordered by the court to stop the nuisance. A director of the company said that 'this decision puts every
greyhound track in the country at jeopardy.'

In giving judgment, Mr Justice Hinchcliffe made some
general remarks about noise in the country. 'When country
dwellers are unable to open a window or to enjoy working,
resting, or pottering about in the garden, when the barking

134

of dogs can be heard above the sound of a washing machine, when rest is interfered with and one has to leave home for peace and quiet – then a substantial nuisance has taken place.'

Under the Noise Abatement Act 1960, persons who cause noise which is a nuisance in the legal sense may in many cases be prosecuted. Noise made deliberately and unnecessarily in order to annoy a neighbour is never justified, however reasonable the noise might be in other circumstances. The leading modern case on deliberate nuisance is *Hollywood Silver Fox Farm v Emmett*.[11]

In September 1934, a Captain Chandler decided to start business as a breeder of silver foxes. He bought a house called Hollywood Cottage, together with twenty acres of land at Kingsdown near Wrotham in Kent, put up a number of pens, and started business with thirteen vixens and twelve dog foxes. Shortly afterwards, he transferred the business to a company which he controlled.

On the north side of the property was a road called School Lane, and on the north-east side of it was a field which belonged to a builder called Emmett. Chandler put up a notice board saying 'Hollywood Silver Fox Farm' facing School Lane, but visible from the field.

Emmett intended to build some bungalows on the field. He had made a private road across the middle of it, and had divided the land on either side into plots. He thought that the notice board would deter people from buying the bungalows, called on Chandler, and asked him to put the notice board somewhere else. Chandler replied bluntly that he could not see any reason for moving it. A few days later, Emmett called again, and repeated his request. Chandler again refused to do anything. On that occasion, Emmett threatened Chandler that if the board were not removed, he would during the breeding season shoot as near as he could get to the breeding pens. 'You will not raise a single cub,' he said.

Silver foxes breed once a year between January and May or early June. During the breeding season, the vixens are extremely nervous, and any loud or unusual noise in the neighbourhood, such as the shooting of guns, is likely to do them injury. Vixens may be put off mating or if they have

135

already mated, may have a miscarriage. Those which have whelped may kill and eat the cubs.

One evening early in April 1935 Emmett carried out his threat. He sent his son to discharge a twelve-bore gun at the boundary of his land nearest to the pens. There was a similar incident on each of the three following evenings. Chandler protested, but Emmett replied that he had a right to shoot as he pleased on his own land. Chandler went to his solicitor, who wrote to Emmett and asked him for an undertaking to stop shooting near the breeding pens. Emmett replied that he was shooting to keep down rabbits. The company then brought proceedings against Emmett, asking for an injunction to stop the nuisance.

By the time the case was heard, it was possible to estimate how much damage had been caused by the shooting. Only nine cubs had been reared during 1935, whereas about thirty ought to have been reared. One of the vixens had eaten her four cubs and others had not mated at all.

Counsel for Emmett argued that shooting to the extent which Emmett had shot was an ordinary incident of the occupation of land and did not amount to a nuisance. 'The plaintiff' he said, 'cannot, because it carries on a business requiring a greater degree of quiet than ordinary uses of land, prevent the defendant from using his land in a way which would not be a nuisance apart from the special uses to which the plaintiff put its land. The shooting,' he continued, 'would have caused no alarm, and done no harm, to the animals which are usually to be found on farms in Kent.' Counsel for the company replied that 'a degree of noise not otherwise actionable may become an actionable nuisance if it is caused maliciously.' Giving judgment, Mr Justice McNaghten said: 'I am satisfied that the defendant sent his son to shoot near the breeding pens, not for the purpose of killing rabbits, but for the purpose of frightening the vixens in the breeding pens, and for no other purpose at all . . . I think that in the circumstances an injunction should be granted restraining the defendant from committing a nuisance by the discharge of firearms or the making of other loud noises in the vicinity of the Hollywood Silver Fox Farm during the breeding season, namely between January 1 and June 15, so as to alarm or disturb the foxes kept by the plaintiff at the said farm, or otherwise to injure the plaintiff company.'

smells and smoke

Smells, and more often smoke, may be a source of annoyance. In the country some smells, for example from hay, from animals, or from insecticides, is normal, and has to be endured. Farmers should do what they can to reduce smells which may affect neighbours, but they cannot be expected to eliminate them entirely.

It is reasonable to light an occasional bonfire in order to burn rubbish, and to set fire to stubble after harvest. On the other hand, the continual belching forth of black smoke from a factory chimney is a serious nuisance against the continuation of which the courts may make an injunction. Whether or not any particular conduct is, or is not, a nuisance is partly a question of reasonableness and part a question of degree.

In the late nineteenth century, there were horse-drawn trams in London. About 1890, the London Tramways Company constructed a tramline along the Balham Road. Just behind that road it built stable blocks in which it could keep up to 440 horses, and where normally about 200 horses were stabled.

A man called Rapier owned a large house in Tooting Park Road, off the Balham Road, and about forty yards from one of the stable blocks. He complained of the smell caused by the horses, and eventually took proceedings for an injunction to stop the company from using the stables in such a way as to be a nuisance to him and his family. The case, under the name of *Rapier v London Tramways Company*,[12] was heard first by the Queen's Bench Division of the High Court and then by the Court of Appeal.

In the Queen's Bench Division, Mr Justice Kekewich gave the injunction. 'The company', he said 'may keep any number of horses . . . but it must do it subject to this, that it must not incommode its neighbours . . . It must either give up the stink or give up the stables.' The company appealed. In the Court of Appeal, Lord Justice

Lindley said of the company that: 'being a company formed for making tramways, it has bought a piece of land near the plaintiff's house, about five acres in extent. It had erected, at very considerable expense, very excellent stables upon this land, capable of holding more than 400 horses . . . All that is perfectly lawful. There is no reason why people should not have stables, and large stables too, provided only they carry on their stable business in such a way as not to occasion a nuisance to their neighbours . . . That being the law applicable to the case, I now pass on to consider the facts. Do the defendants so carry on their business as to commit a nuisance . . . Do they create in the conduct of their business such a smell as diminishes the reasonable enjoyment and comfort of the plaintiff's house? The fact that somebody with a sensitive nose smells some ammonia and does not like it will not prove a nuisance; it is a question of degree. You can only appeal to the common sense of ordinary people. The test is whether the smell is so bad and continuous as seriously to interfere with comfort and enjoyment.'

Lord Justice Lindley found that the smell was both bad and continuous. 'The result is that we cannot disturb the order which has been made . . . What that may involve I cannot possibly say . . . If the company cannot have 200 horses together, even when it takes proper precautions, without committing a nuisance, all I can say is that it cannot have so many horses together. No doubt it is a serious matter to the company but I cannot bring my mind to say that I disagree with the learned judge who tried the case in the court below.'

Smoke and fumes from industrial districts occasionally cause damage to property in nearby rural areas. The courts will not, however, hold a particular industrial undertaking liable unless the landowner can prove, beyond reasonable doubt, that the damage was caused by the operations of that undertaking.

In the old case of *Salvin v North Brancepeth Coal Company*,[13] Salvin owned a country house and 485 acres of land at Burnshall, Durham. There were many collieries on all sides of the estate. Some of them had been worked for thirty or forty years. In 1870, the company opened a new pit 1,000 yards from the house and only 400 yards from one of the plantations. It put up a large number of coke ovens near the pit. Salvin alleged that the smoke and fumes emitted by the ovens were causing damage to his fields and woods. He brought proceedings for an injunction to stop the company 'from allowing any effluvia to issue from its works so as to occasion nuisance to him or diminish the value of his estate'. The company replied that there were a large number of other colleries and coke ovens in the neighbourhood. The smoke and fumes produced by their own ovens did not add perceptibly to the pollution of an already polluted atmosphere.

The court refused to make the injunction, 'The plaintiff', said Lord Justice James 'has utterly failed to make out his case. There was no proved instance of a single tree killed or substantially injured, or of a single blade of grass burnt or destroyed.'

When industrial operations cause excessive smoke or fumes, the persons responsible may be prosecuted under the Public Health Act 1936 or the Clean Air Act 1956.

Scotland

There are no important differences.

Northern Ireland

There are no important differences.

Notes to this chapter are on page 190.

9 Commons

The word 'common' originally referred to the way in which land was used, by people in common. It was not until much later that the word was applied to the land itself.

The Angles and Saxons and the other invaders of Britain gradually settled down in permanent communities. To begin with, the country was sparsely populated, and agriculture was very primitive. The new inhabitants were able to till only a tiny part of the land. They left the rest open and uncultivated. In so far as they used it at all, they did so in common, the woodlands as a source of fuel, and the wastelands to provide fodder and grazing.

As the centuries passed, the population increased and agriculture became more advanced, the commonland came under the control of the lords of the manor. Slowly they began to cultivate it, and enclose it with hedges, compensating the dispossessed peasants by giving them allotments. The use of the commons which still existed had to be restricted: a ceiling might be put on the number of animals a man could turn out to graze, and on the amount of fodder and fuel he was entitled to collect. Rights of common still exist.

proving a right

A person can prove that he has a right of common in one of two ways. He can produce a written document in his favour. Alternatively, he can prove that he lives on the land of a manor, that the common is in the same manor, and that he and his predecessors had exercised the right since 'time immemorial'. In practice, however, it may be enough to show that he and possibly the previous occupants of his house have used the local common for their horses, say, without objection for a number of years.

White v Taylor[1] is a notable recent case on rights of common. White and others owned farmlands at Martin, in Hampshire. Taylor owned Martin Down, which was formerly commonland of the manor of Martin. White claimed a right to keep sheep on the down, and other subsidiary rights. Taylor contested his claim.

The case was long and complicated. As Mr Justice Buckley said, 'this action is about grazing . . . rights over a down in Hampshire. It has been fought with a pertinacity and vigour which says much for the powers of endurance of the breed of Hampshire sheep farmers to which the plaintiff belongs.' After much involved argument, Mr Justice Buckley decided that White, as owner of land in the former manor had a right to keep sheep on the down. He also decided that he had other subsidiary rights.

'The defendant contended that it could not be necessary for those plaintiffs who are entitled to sheep rights and have land adjoining the down to have troughs on the down, because they could install watering facilities on their own land which would be available to sheep on the down. I do not accept this argument . . . Watering facilities at one point on the edge of the down would be unlikely to be of much, if any value, when sheep were grazing on a remote part of the down'. The plaintiffs, therefore, had a right to put troughs on the down wherever it was reasonably necessary to do so. 'Anyone having a right to depasture sheep on the down (that is to say, to use the down for sheep grazing) must also incidentally be entitled to go on to the down, either himself or . . . his shepherd, to do anything necessary for the proper care and management of the sheep. But this does not mean that the owner of the sheep rights can drive anywhere on the down in a vehicle. There may be occasions when it will be necessary to take a vehicle on to the down . . . for the purpose of doing something necessary in connection with the sheep on the down; but where the use of a vehicle would not be necessary for purposes connected with the welfare of the sheep and would be merely a convenience for someone in the vehicle, such use would not, in my judgment, be permissible.'

Commons Registration Act 1965

Under the Commons Registration Act 1965 all common-land, town or village greens, rights of common, and the ownership of commonland must now be registered in most cases in the country with the appropriate county council. Town or village greens are defined as 'land which has been allocated by or under any Act for the exercise or recreation of the inhabitants of any locality or on which the inhabitants of any locality have a customary right to indulge in lawful sports and pastimes or on which the inhabitants of any locality have indulged in such sports or pastimes as of right for not less than twenty years.'[2]

rights of commoners

Persons who have a right to make special use of a common are called commoners. The right which is most often exercised is called the 'common of pasture'. People who have horses or ponies, but no fields of their own to keep them in, frequently put them out to graze on a nearby common. Some farmers exercise the right by putting cattle out on commons. In a few places, like the New Forest, pigs are turned out on wooded commonland to feed on beech mast and acorns; the right is then known as 'pannage'.

The other rights of common, though found much less often, do still exist. The 'common of estovers' is a right of the commoner to take wood for the repair of his house and for fuel. The 'common of turbary' is a right to take turf or peat from commonland for use as fuel. The 'common of piscary' is a right to fish in any streams or ponds on the common, and the 'common in the soil' is a right to take sand, gravel, or stone for household use. If commonland is compulsorily purchased, for housing or to make a new road for example, the commoners are entitled to be compensated for the loss of their rights.

142

Commoners also have a right to remove obstructions from their commons, as the case of *R v Dyer*[3] showed. Dyer and others were commoners of a common at Winford in Somerset. The Winford Parish Council allowed a company carrying out building works in the neighbourhood to erect a board on the common with an arrow pointing to the building site. The commoners removed the board and damaged the supports. The company reported the matter to the police, and the police charged the commoners with malicious damage. At Somerset Quarter Sessions, the commoners were convicted and given conditional discharges.

The commoners appealed against conviction to the Court of Criminal Appeal. The court quashed the conviction. The judges said that the notice board was a trespass on the common, which the commoners were entitled to abate. The parish council had no power to allow the company to erect a board, and the commoners were at liberty to remove it.

rights of the lord of the manor

The lord of the manor is the owner of the soil of many commons in rural areas. Broadly speaking, he can exercise all the rights of the commoners, though not to such an extent that they are unable to exercise their rights. In addition, he can shoot game there.

He is entitled to compensation in the event of the compulsory purchase of the common or part of it.

rights of the public

The Law of Property Act 1925 gives to the public rights of access for air and exercise to commons in London and other urban areas. Lords of the manor have given similar rights to the public over some rural commons. It is, however, an offence to park a motor vehicle on a common except within fifteen yards of a road.[4]

Scotland

The only common ground in Scotland is in crofting communities.

Northern Ireland

Generally speaking, the only common land in Northern Ireland is hill sheep-grazing land. There are no provisions as to registration of commons. The only legislation in force is two Acts of the old Irish parliament: they prohibit the destruction of the surface of commons except for the taking of turf, and require that pigs put on common land have rings in their noses.[5]

Notes to this chapter are on page 190.

10 Agriculture and Forestry

For some years after the second world war, the Minister of Agriculture and Fisheries[1] had almost despotic powers. If land was not being properly farmed, he could force the farmer to sell it. Even more humiliating, he could make a supervision order under which the farmer was told exactly what to do and what not to do. These extreme powers were abolished by the Agriculture Act 1958. Today, the main function of the Minister of Agriculture, Fisheries and Food is to advise and assist the farmer.

A large number of official bodies assist the minister. There is for example a National Agricultural Advisory Service to give technical advice and help. Then there is a Central Council for Agricultural and Horticultural Co-operation to help farmers to pool their resources in production, storage, marketing, and the provision of buildings and equipment. There is a Meat and Livestock Commission to promote greater efficiency in the production and sale of meat. There are marketing boards for the sale of agricultural products. The minister delegates many powers to country agricultural executive committees. In addition, agricultural tribunals have been appointed, their duty being to decide certain disputes arising between farmers and their landlords.

rural development boards

Rural development boards have an important part to play in the countryside. The Minister of Agriculture, Fisheries and Food and the Secretary of State for Wales[2] 'for meeting the special problems of the development as rural areas of hills and uplands, and the special need of such areas may . . . establish a board, to be known as a rural development board, for any area appearing to be one where those problems or needs exist.'

The main function of a rural development board is to make agriculture profitable. This may mean, for example, advising on the best use of land and giving assistance in the amalgamation of small units. A board must however always bear in mind 'the need for preserving and taking full advantage of the amenities and scenery . . . in the course of . . . development . . .' The amenities include 'any feature of scientific or historic interest . . . flora and fauna and physiographical features, and any buildings of special interest.'

Rural development boards have power to acquire farms and other land by agreement, and to carry out enquiries and investigations. They may make grants and loans towards the expense of installing supplies of water, gas, or electricity in cottages and towards the cost of providing camping or caravan sites for visitors.

There are special restrictions on the planting of trees in the area of a rural development board. Normally it is necessary to obtain a licence from the board.[3]

grants for farmers

The Minister of Agriculture Fisheries and Food[4] may make grants of many different kinds to farmers. Some of the grants are for work which may greatly affect the appearance of the countryside.

Under ploughing-grants schemes, for example, grants may be made in respect of the ploughing-up of land which has been under grass for a specified minimum period. The payment of grants may be made subject to conditions. A typical condition may specify a minimum area to be ploughed up. Grants may also be paid for the renovation of land which has been under grass for a minimum specified period.[5]

Again, under livestock-rearing land-improvement schemes, improvement grants may be made to turn moorland into livestock-rearing land. Livestock-rearing land is defined as 'land situated in an area consisting predominantly of mountains, hills or heath, being land which is, or by improvement could be made, suitable for use for the breeding, rearing, and maintenance of sheep or cattle, but not for carrying on, to any material extent, of dairy farming, or for the production, to any material extent, of fat sheep or fat cattle, or for the production of crops in quantity materially greater than that necessary to feed the number of sheep or cattle capable of being maintained on the land.'

Improvements which may qualify for grants include the making and improvement of roads, and fences, the reclaiming of waste land and the establishment of shelter belts, the laying down of permanent pasture, the regeneration of grazings, the burning of heather or grass, and the erection and alteration of farm buildings, farm houses or cottages.[6]

farm animals

A licence or a permit from the minister is necessary before certain animals can be kept. The animals in question are stallions aged two years or more, bulls aged ten months or more, and boars aged six months or more. The minister must normally grant a licence unless the animal is diseased or has some defect rendering it unsuitable for breeding. When he is not completely satisfied about the suitability of an animal he may grant a permit subject to conditions. If an animal is kept without a licence or permit, the minister may order it to be destroyed.[7]

In order to improve the quality of sheep, the minister may make regulations controlling the keeping of rams in certain areas. He may require rams to be marked and approved for breeding. He may order them to be slaughtered or castrated when he considers them unsuitable for breeding. Persons contravening the regulations may be prosecuted.[8]

tenant farmers

A tenant farmer has a duty to his landlord to cultivate the

land 'in a husbandlike manner.' Provided he fulfils this duty, he is well protected by the law.

Agricultural land, except for grazing or mowing, cannot be let for very short periods. If an attempt to let agricultural land for a year or less is made, a tenancy from year to year is created. This means that the tenancy continues until notice to quit is given. A notice to quit must give the farmer at least twelve months from the end of the current year of the tenancy. A tenancy of agricultural land for two years or more continues automatically after the end of the lease as a tenancy from year to year. If the landlord wishes to end the tenancy when the lease expires, he must give the farmer notice to quit between one and two years beforehand.

A farmer who receives a notice to quit is normally entitled to serve a counter-notice on the landlord. There are, however, a few exceptions, for example where the land has been farmed badly, or where the landlord has obtained planning permission to build houses on the land.

If the farmer does serve a valid counter-notice, the notice to quit becomes null and void unless the agricultural land tribunal for the area consents to its operation. The tribunal must not give consent unless the landlord has a specified ground for wanting possession. The more important of the specified grounds are that the termination of the tenancy is desirable in the interests of good husbandry, that the land is required for some purpose which is not agricultural, or that the hardship to the landlord if consent were refused would be greater than the hardship to the tenant if consent were granted.

A recent case on hardship is *Purser v Bailey*.[9] Two farms at Therfield in Hertfordshire were let by Bailey to Purser in 1955. In 1959, Purser bought one of these from Bailey. He ran both farms as a single unit throughout. Bailey died in 1965, and under his will he gave £1,000 to his widow, and £500 to each of his two daughters. The farm, however, was heavily mortgaged, and the interest on the mortgage was much greater than the rent paid by Purser. If the farm were sold, the mortgage could be paid off, and there would be a surplus from which to pay the legacies. The widow was living on national assistance and was in great need of the money.

Purser was given notice to quit. He served a counter-notice on the executor. The case came before the Agricultural Land Tribunal, Eastern Area, which gave consent to the operation of the notice to quit. It said that the hardship to the widow and daughters if consent were not given outweighed the hardship which would be caused to Purser by the giving of consent.

Purser appealed, arguing that it was not refusal of consent which would cause hardship to Mrs Bailey. The hardship had already been caused to her by the state in which Bailey had left his affairs. The court rejected this. 'In my judgment', said Lord Denning, 'the tribunal can consider the hardship on each side with regard to all the attendant circumstances . . . No doubt it is hard for the tenant to have to go; but after all he did buy the other farm, and I expect he will be one of the possible purchasers of this farm if it is sold.'

Oddly enough, the special rules as to notices do not apply where agricultural land is let for more than a year but less than two years. In one case, Lord Denning expressed surprise that Parliament had not filled this obvious gap.

A tenant farmer who quits is normally entitled to be compensated by his landlord for the growing crops which he leaves behind and for the improvements which he has made during his tenancy. He may also be entitled to compensation for disturbance.[10]

farm cottages

On many farms and country estates cottages for the workers go with the job. When a worker leaves his employment, the employer normally needs the cottage for a new worker.

In the past, the right of an employee to occupy his cottage ended on the day when his notice expired, and if he remained there he had no legal protection whatever. The employer was entitled to evict him and his family, and to remove all his belongings, with force if necessary. The employer could call upon the court and its officials for prompt assistance if the employee was troublesome, or if the employer did not wish to carry out the actual eviction himself.

Those days have gone. If an employee who has left his job refuses to leave his cottage, the employer must apply to the court for an order for possession. Provided that the employer requires the cottage for another employee, the order is normally granted. Having made an order, however, the court may suspend its execution for a period or periods. In considering whether to suspend, the court must take all the circumstances into account. Three criteria are of particular importance :

'(a) whether other suitable accommodation is or can be made available to the occupier.

(b) whether the efficient management of any agricultural land or the efficient carrying on of any agricultural operations would be seriously prejudiced unless the premises were available for occupation by a person employed or to be employed by the owner, and

(c) whether greater hardship would be caused by the suspension of the order than by its execution without suspension or further suspension.'

Where an order is made within six months of the end of a tenancy, the court must normally suspend it at least until the six months expire.

It is a serious offence to evict, or to attempt to evict, an old employee from a farm or estate cottage.[11]

the Forestry Commission

The Forestry Commission was established in 1919. The objects of the commission are 'promoting the interests of forestry, the development of afforestation and the production and supply of timber and other forest products in Great Britain.' The commission must promote the establishment and maintenance of adequate reserves of growing trees. Woods and forests which are not privately owned, are for the most part owned by the Ministry of Agriculture, Fisheries and Food, but the commission has the control and management of them.[12]

The commission has wide powers. It may buy and sell trees and wood; it may establish and carry on woodland industries;

t may carry out research into forestry and publish the results; and it may establish training schools for foresters. It must prepare an annual report, which must be laid before Parliament.

It has power to make orders compelling the owners and occupiers of land to allow timber to be hauled across the land, on payment of rent and compensation for damage done. Officers of the commission may enter and survey land to ascertain its suitability for afforestation. With Treasury approval, the commission may make grants or loans for afforestation or replanting of trees.

It is empowered, with respect to any land under its management or control to which the public may have access, to make bylaws for the preservation of trees, timber, and amenities, and for regulating the use of the land by the public. Drafts of bylaws must be laid before Parliament for not less than forty days before the bylaws are due to come into operation.

Bylaws must not affect anyone's rights of common without the consent of that person. No bylaw for the Forest of Dean or the New Forest may be made except after consultation with the verderers concerned. Officers of the commission have authority to enforce the bylaws, and in particular, they may remove or exclude persons suspected of committing offences against the bylaws.

Under the Countryside Act 1968, the commission may provide certain facilities on land managed by them, these being accommodation for visitors, camping sites, places for meals and refreshments, picnic places, places for enjoying views, parking places, nature study trails and footpaths, information and display centres, shops in connection with these facilities, and public conveniences. The commission may make such charges as it thinks fit for their use.[13]

felling of trees

In general, no person may fell any growing tree without a licence by the Forestry Commission authorising the felling. (Felling includes wilfully destroying by any means). But the exceptions are many and important, and include:

151

1 the topping or lopping of trees or the trimming or laying of hedges;
2 the felling of trees of a diameter not exceeding three inches or, in the case of coppice or underwood, of a diameter not exceeding six inches;
3 the felling of any fruit trees or any trees standing or growing on land comprised in an orchard, garden, churchyard or public open space;
4 the felling of any tree for the prevention of danger or the prevention or abatement of a nuisance;
5 the felling, by any person, of trees of a diameter not exceeding four inches on land in his occupation, or in the occupation of his tenant, where the felling is carried out in order to improve the growth of other trees;
6 the felling by any person of trees on land in his occupation or in the occupation of his tenant, so long as the aggregate cubic content of the trees to be felled without a licence does not exceed 825 cubic feet in any quarter, and the aggregate cubic content of the trees so felled which are sold by that person, whether before or after the felling, does not exceed 150 cubic feet in any quarter or such large quantity as the Forestry Commission may in any particular case allow.

As a general rule the commission must grant licences and must grant them unconditionally. However, if the commission thinks it expedient in the interests of good forestry, or agriculture, or the amenities of a district, it may either refuse to grant a licence, or grant it subject to conditions.

When the commission proposes to impose conditions, it asks the applicant for his views about the proposed conditions. Conditions may require the replanting of land on which the felling is to take place, or the planting of other land nearby. They may also require the maintenance of the new trees in accordance with the rules and practice of good forestry for up to ten years.

If the commission refuses to grant a licence, or proposes to make conditions, the applicant can generally require the decision to be reviewed by a special appeal committee of three. The members of the committee are chosen by the minister after consultation with organisations representing the owners of woodlands and timber merchants. The committee must give an opportunity both to the commission and the applicant to put their respective points of view. The committee must then send a report to the minister who may confirm, reverse, or modify the decision of the commission.

When an application for a felling licence is refused, the owner of the tree may require the commission to pay compensation if, in the future, the quality of the timber deteriorates and the value of the tree falls as a result of that deterioration. Claims may be made from time to time, as deterioration takes place. The commission may, however, at any time reverse its previous decision and grant a felling licence. If it does this, the amount of compensation is limited to the fall in value up to the date when it informs the applicant that a licence has been granted.

The commission has power to compel, as well as to prevent, the felling of trees. When the commission believes it to be in the interests of good forestry that a tree should be felled, it may serve a notice on the owner. The notice directs him to have the tree felled within a certain period which must, however, be not less than two years.

Notices may be served on two grounds. One ground is to prevent deterioration, or further deterioration, in the timber of the tree to be felled. The other ground is to improve the growth of nearby trees. In considering whether to serve a notice, the commission must have regard to the interests of agriculture and the amenity or convenience of any farm or house, or park surrounding a house. The commission has no power to serve notices requiring the felling of any fruit trees, or any trees standing or growing in a garden, churchyard, or public open space.

An owner who receives a felling direction may appeal to the minister within three months. Appeals are referred to the special appeal committee which makes a report to the minister. He may confirm, modify, or withdraw the felling direction in accordance with the report of the committee.

When a landowner suffers loss as a result of a felling direction, he may require the Forestry Commission to buy the trees, or the minister to buy the land.

Anyone who fells a tree without a licence in a case where

153

one is necessary is guilty of an offence, for which he may be prosecuted. When a person fails to obey a felling direction or to observe a condition in a felling licence the commission may serve a notice of default on him. If he does not do what is required, the commission may do the work itself at his expense. In addition, he may be prosecuted.[14]

Scotland

There are no important differences.

Northern Ireland

County committees of agriculture carry out many of the same functions as county agricultural executive committees in England and Wales. There are no agricultural tribunals.

There are no rural development boards. The Ministry of Commerce, however, has rural industries and local enterprise development committees which advise on the development of country areas.

In the nineteenth century, insecurity of tenure and unfair rents were a great source of bitterness amongst tenant farmers.

A large body of legislation to deal with these grievances was passed in the second half of the century. The legislation is still generally in force, giving protection from eviction to tenants and providing compensation for improvements when they leave.

The Forestry Division of the Northern Ireland Ministry of Agriculture is responsible for forests and has wide powers similar to those of the Forestry Commission. Many of the state forests have facilities for visitors.

No compensation is payable if a felling licence is refused.

Notes to this chapter are on page 191.

11 Rates

Rates are the oldest tax still being collected in this country. Their origin lies far back in the Middle Ages, but modern rating really started with the Poor Relief Act of 1601. During the nineteenth century, rates were imposed to cover other important local needs like roads, street lighting, public health, police and education. Except for water rates, all these local taxes are now consolidated in the general rates levied by the local authorities.

Rates are paid by the occupiers of land. The general idea is that the occupation of land is a valuable right, worth so much a year. Every year each council fixes the amount in the pound to be paid by the ratepayers in its area. If, for example, a property has a rateable value of £100 per year, and the council fixes the poundage for the year at 65p, the amount payable in that year will be £65.

Originally, the councils also valued properties for rating, but there were complaints of lack of uniformity in valuations. In 1948, therefore, the system was centralised. Responsibility for valuation was transferred to the Board of Inland Revenue, which established its own valuation offices throughout the country.

liability for rates

Rates must be paid in respect of all land and houses unless the property is of a class specifically exempted from liability. Crown property, churches, and some schools are exempt from rates. The most important exemption, however, is agricultural land and agricultural buildings.[1]

agricultural land and agricultural buildings

Agricultural land is defined as 'any land used as arable, meadow, or pasture ground only, and land used for a plantation or a wood for the growth of saleable underwood, land exceeding one quarter of an acre used for the purpose of poultry farming, cottage gardens exceeding one quarter of an acre, market gardens, nursery grounds, orchards, or allotments.' It does not include land occupied together with a house as a park, gardens other than market or allotment gardens, pleasure grounds, land kept or preserved mainly or exclusively for the purposes of sport or recreation, or land used as a racecourse.[2]

There are many borderline cases. *Jarvis v Cambridgeshire Assessment Committee*[3] was a typical one. Jarvis was a farmer, who owned a field of about twelve acres and used it to grow crops until he was approached by a man called Dawson who trained racehorses. Dawson asked him to put the field down to grass and let it out for the training of horses, and Jarvis did this. Most of the horse-training in fact took place elsewhere, and Dawson used the field each year from Christmas to the beginning of March only. At other times Jarvis used it for grazing or haymaking, or for exercising two of his own horses.

The valuation officer contended that as the land was not 'used as arable meadow or pasture ground only' and was 'kept or preserved mainly or exclusively for purposes of sport or recreation' it was not agricultural property. He further contended that as Dawson used the property for training racehorses, and enjoyed the exclusive use of it for part of the year for that purpose, Dawson was in rateable occupation of the land. The ratepayers replied that the land was 'used as meadow or pasture ground only' and was 'not kept or preserved mainly for sport or recreation'. The court, in a very short judgment, decided that the ratepayers were right. The main use of the property was agricultural and the property was therefore entitled to exemption from rates.

An agricultural building is a building 'occupied together with agricultural land' and 'used solely in connection with agricultural operations carried out on agricultural land'.[4] The question whether a particular building is an agricultural building within this definition can be extremely difficult.

The case of *National Pig-Progeny Testing Board v Greenall*[5] concerned the rateability of a pig-progeny testing station at Hambleton in the West Riding of Yorkshire. The station consisted of a building costing over £100,000 in which 400 young pigs were reared under strictly controlled conditions, on food carefully regulated and measured, until they reached a certain weight. There was also nearly seven acres of land which was a wilderness of weeds and rubble when taken over by the board. The board had ploughed and harrowed the land twice, but had not decided what to do with it; corn might be grown or the land might be put to grass. If corn were grown, the straw could be used for bedding in the building. If grass were grown, testing operations could be carried out on pigs kept out of doors.

The board contended that the station was agricultural property. The valuation officer, however, argued that the land was not agricultural land because it was not 'land used as arable, meadow, or pasture ground only'. The building was not, therefore, 'used solely in connection with agricultural operations carried out on agricultural land'.

Lord Justice Harman, delivering judgment in the Court of Appeal, said that the land passed the test as agricultural land. 'A decision had been made to put it to an agricultural use. It had been ploughed and harrowed, operations essential to that end . . . The fact that the owners had not decided to which agricultural use it should be put does not seem to us fatal'. Turning to the buildings, he went on: 'They must pass two tests. First they must be "occupied together with agricultural land" and second they must be "used solely in connection with agricultural operations thereon . . ." These buildings are occupied together with the land which we have held to be agricultural land. They therefore pass the first test. The use to which the buildings are put is clear. It is the raising of pigs. True, these are not raised in the normal commercial way and the object is not to make a profit but to collect statistical information for the help of farmers. Nevertheless it seems clear to us that this is an agricultural operation.

'The crucial point is whether this use is connected solely

with agricultural operations on the land. In our judgment, the ratepayers' case breaks down at this point. The use of the building . . . appears to us to have had no connection at all with any agricultural operations on the land. Those operations had not gone beyond the stage of ploughing and it was quite uncertain what the future might bring.' The building was not, therefore, an agricultural building within the definition and the board lost its case.

W. & J. B. Eastwood Ltd v Herrod (Valuation Officer)[6] was another difficult case, and was taken to the House of Lords. The company produced broiler chickens on an 1,150 acre farm. The seventy-two broiler houses could each hold 22,000 birds, which were kept there throughout their lives. The rest of the land was used to grow barley, which provided a very small part of the food for the birds.

The company contended that the broiler houses were exempt from rates because they were agricultural buildings. The valuation officer argued that the buildings were industrial buildings. The House of Lords decided that the valuation officer was right. Lord Reid remarked that the exemption from rates of agricultural land 'was intended to benefit agriculturists but not those conducting commercial enterprises when the use of agricultural land plays only a small part in the enterprise'. Lord Guest said that: 'the buildings are used for the growing of chickens bought in which are fed to a very large extent on bought in foodstuffs . . . The operation carried on in the broiler houses and associated buildings is in my opinion an independent and separate commercial operation from that which was carried on on the land. The buildings fall to be rated.'

The Rating Act 1971 exempts from rates some buildings which would have been rateable according to these decisions. Broadly speaking these are buildings used solely for the keeping or breeding of livestock, which stand in at least five acres of agricultural land.

the valuation of property

The rateable value of property, broadly speaking, is the rent at which it might be let for a year in an ideal open market.[7] Comparable properties which have already been valued provide a good guide. If there are no comparable properties, however, the calculation of the rateable value may be a task of great complexity.

The property may not be let at all, and in some cases there may be no market, or only a very restricted market, for it. On the other hand there may be a great shortage of properties for letting so that the rents are artificially high. But even if there is a free market for that kind of property, and even if it is actually let, the rent may be little guide to the rateable value. The terms of the letting, for example, may not conform exactly to the specified pattern, or the property may not be in the reasonable state of repair which must be assumed. As a judge said in 1960, in valuing property for rates 'we are in a world of make believe'.

Valuation of all properties liable to rates is carried out every few years by officials appointed by the Board of Inland Revenue. A ratepayer is not bound to accept the assessment of the valuation officer: if he thinks it is too high, he can appeal to the local valuation court. From there, both sides can appeal to the Lands Tribunal, and eventually, on a question of law, to the Court of Appeal.[8]

The appeal case of *Surrey County Valuation Committee v Chessington Zoo Ltd*,[9] shows how the rateable value of an unusual property in the country may be greatly increased by a change in the basis of valuation. In 1948 the rateable value of Chessington Zoo was assessed at £663 on the basis that it was simply a country house in parkland. The valuation officer proposed to raise it to £8,000 on the footing that a flourishing business was carried on there. The company appealed. The court decided that a very considerable increase in the rateable value was justified. Lord Goddard said that:

'In valuing such a hereditament, it seems to me, no assistance whatever can be derived by ascertaining what a tenant would be likely to pay as rent for a country mansion with park attached which he intended to use as a private residence . . . I think we ought to look at the position as though a landowner had premises to offer equipped for a zoo and amusement park which a person carrying on that class of business wished to take.'

159

valuation of sporting rights

Agricultural land does not include woods kept wholly or mainly for sporting. Where land, or a river, is used by the owner wholly or mainly for sport, the owner must pay rates on it. If he lets the shooting or fishing rights, the rates may be payable either by the landlord, or the tenant as occupier, depending on the circumstances. Sometimes a tenant who pays rates for sporting has a right to deduct a proportion of them from his rent, but the rules are rather complicated.

The main factor in valuing sporting rights is the number of animals, fish or birds on the property. But there are also other factors, such as the general nature of the country, the conditions of the coverts and woodlands, the extent of disturbing influence such as roads, the facilities for proper keepering, and to some extent the degree of infestation by vermin. Fashionable shoots and rivers have a higher value than those which are unfashionable.[10]

Scotland

There are no important differences, rating being fixed by local authorities. There is quinquennial valuation reckoned from 1961.

Northern Ireland

There are no important differences.

Notes to this chapter are on page 191.

12 Inns

An inn is defined as 'an establishment held out by the proprietor as offering food, drink, and, if so required, sleeping
accommodation, without special contract, to any traveller
presenting himself who appears able and willing to pay a
reasonable sum for the services and facilities provided and
who is in a fit state to be received.'[1] Many inns are small
country pubs which provide meals at the bar and have
a few rooms for residents. At the other end of the scale,
luxurious hotels in London and other cities may also be
inns.

Lodging houses, guest houses, boarding houses and hotels
which describe themselves as private hotels are not inns.
Though a public house may be called an inn, it is not in fact
an inn unless it offers sleeping accommodation and meals as
well as drink. Inns usually have inn or hotel signs outside,
but they do not have to display signs.

travellers

An innkeeper does not have to receive anyone who is not
a 'traveller'. The word 'traveller' has a very wide meaning
and may include a person living quite close to the inn, as the
case of *Williams v Linnitt*[2] showed. Williams lived at Caldecote near Nuneaton in Warwickshire. One evening, he called
for a drink at the Royal Red Gate Inn, Watling Street, about
a mile from Caldecote. Whilst he was drinking, his car was
stolen. At that time (1951) an innkeeper was liable for the
safety of the property of travellers using his inn and the question arose as to whether Williams was a traveller. The court

L   161

decided that he was. Lord Justice Asquith, in his judgment, said:

'I think that the meaning of the word traveller has in the course of time undergone some modification. According to decisions in Tudor and Stuart times, there might have been some warrant for restricting it to persons who resorted to the inn for accommodation for the night. However long this notion endured, it received its quietus when an eighteenth century case decided that a man who, on his way home from Manchester market, entered an inn, and had his goods stolen whilst having a drink, was entitled to the special remedies against an innkeeper, there being no question of his lodging at the inn for the night . . . So again in a nineteenth century case, the plaintiff was held entitled to enforce the special obligations resting on an innkeeper when he stopped at the inn for a meal when en route from his office in Liverpool to his residence some miles outside it. I cannot persuade myself, that if this is so, a person who travels to an inn from his own residence for a meal or a drink and travels back to his own residence afterwards is not a "traveller" also.'

However, Lord Justice Asquith continued, 'the term "traveller" even on this broad construction, is very far from embracing all comers: it excludes, for instance: (a) the innkeeper's family living in the inn, (b) the innkeeper's servants, (c) the innkeeper's private guests, (d) lodgers at the inn, and (e) persons resorting to the inn for purposes unconnected with the enjoyment of the facilities which it provides as an inn, for example to repair the drains or to sell the innkeeper a sewing machine.'

cars and other belongings

An innkeeper is bound to accommodate the car in which a traveller arrives if he has garage or parking space. He is also bound to find space for the luggage of a traveller provided that the luggage is of a normal character, and is not dangerous or otherwise objectionable. He must not refuse to take a dog unless the dog is ferocious, though he need not accommodate the dog in the inn itself if there is a suitable outhouse.

children

An innkeeper is bound to accommodate the children of travellers, however young the children may be. The innkeeper is not entitled to refuse to take children on the ground, for example, that the other guests are elderly and would be disturbed by young children. He is not, however, obliged to provide special facilities for children, such as cots and cribs, napkin-drying facilities, or special meals.

right to refuse accommodation or meals

The normal rule is that an innkeeper must not refuse to accommodate a traveller. However, there are circumstances in which he may legitimately refuse. The fact that the bedrooms are all taken is a reasonable ground for refusing to provide a traveller with shelter for the night. A traveller cannot demand to sleep in the lounge or bar, as the case of *Browne v Brandt*[3] showed.

In April 1901 Browne was driving from Crawley in Sussex to London. The car broke down on the way, and Browne walked to an inn called The Chequers at Horley, where he arrived just before two in the morning. He roused Brandt and demanded beds for himself and the friend who was travelling with him. Brandt refused, saying that the inn was full. Browne said that he and his friend would be satisfied if they were allowed to spend the night in the coffee-room. Brandt refused to allow this, saying that he never allowed anyone to sit up all night in the coffee-room. Browne and his friend then left.

They could not get accommodation at another inn, and ultimately Browne hired a taxi to take them back to Crawley. Browne sued Brandt for damages.

In evidence it was said that there were six bedrooms at the inn, and on the night in question three of them were occupied by guests, and three of them by Brandt and his family and employees. The coffee-room and a public sitting-room were not used or occupied on that night.

The court decided that Brandt had not unreasonably

refused to accommodate Browne and his friend. Lord Alverstone said that:

'I cannot think that the authorities to which we have been referred show that where an innkeeper provides a certain number of bedrooms and sitting rooms for the accommodation of guests he is under a legal obligation to receive and shelter as many people as can be put into the rooms without overcrowding. I think a person who comes to the inn has no legal right to demand to pass the night in a public sitting room if the bedrooms are all full, and I think that the landlord has no obligation to receive him.'

A traveller is not entitled to demand to sleep in a particular bedroom in an inn even though the bedroom is vacant.

An innkeeper may legitimately refuse to take a traveller on the ground that he is likely to be a nuisance to other guests. In one case the court held that an innkeeper was justified in turning away a traveller who arrived with a dangerous dog. In another case an innkeeper was held to be justified in turning away a man who was drunk. The most interesting case, however, is probably *Rothfield v North British Railway Company*,[4] which was heard by a Scottish Court. The decision reached is almost certainly good law in England and Wales as well as in Scotland.

Rothfield was a moneylender who had been in the habit of staying at the North British Station Hotel in Edinburgh for two or three nights a week during the first world war. The report says that 'he made himself very conspicuous in the hotel. He did his utmost to attract attention to himself. The other guests quickly got to know who and what he was. And the guests expressed their surprise to one of the directors of the hotel company, and to the manager of the hotel, that such a person was tolerated in the place. Among the residents in the hotel during 1916 and 1917 were large numbers of naval and military officers. Two of the directors and the manager said that Rothfield constantly associated with officers. This troubled the directors who came to think that he was using the hotel for the purpose of promoting his money-lending business.'

In January 1918, Rothfield received a letter from the

manager of the hotel asking him to leave his room on the following day, and not to return to the hotel again. He brought an action against the hotel company, claiming a declaration that as a traveller to Edinburgh he was entitled to be accommodated at the hotel. The court refused to make the declaration. Lord Ormidale said that 'Rothfield had become notorious and an object of suspicion and offence to the other guests, and according to the best judgment the directors could form he was endeavouring to use their premises for operating his business. It would not be reasonable, it seems to me, to exact from them absolute proof that their suspicions were well-founded. It is enough that it clearly appears that they had reasonable grounds for thinking as they did and that they did not act rashly or capriciously, but on the contrary came to an honest conclusion only after patient and anxious consideration of the whole circumstances. On this evidence I think that their contention that they were justified in refusing to receive Rothfield into their hotel is well-founded.'

After a person has stayed in an inn for some days or weeks, depending on the facts of the case, he ceases to be a traveller and becomes a lodger. The innkeeper may then refuse to accommodate him any longer, and may turn him out on giving him reasonable notice.

An innkeeper may not refuse to accommodate a traveller simply because he arrives late or on a Sunday. But however late it is, he need not release a room which another guest has booked unless he told the guest that he would only be reserving it to a particular hour, and that hour has passed. He may not refuse to accommodate a traveller who will not give his name and address. It is, however, the duty of innkeepers, and the keepers of private hotels and guesthouses, to require any person over the age of sixteen who stays there to sign a statement as to his nationality and, in the case of a foreigner, also to give particulars of his name, nationality, date of arrival, passport, and last address.[5]

An innkeeper generally speaking must not refuse to provide a meal and a drink for a traveller. If a traveller demands water with his meal, he is entitled to have it. In an Irish case, an innkeeper was held to have acted without reasonable excuse when one of his waiters refused to serve a traveller who insisted on wearing his overcoat at the table. Of course, if the guest arrives late, when the kitchen staff have gone off duty, the meal need not be very elaborate. That there is no food, or that the available food has been reserved for those who have booked tables is, however, a legitimate excuse for not producing a meal. The innkeeper is not obliged to send out for food.

An innkeeper who *unlawfully* refuses to provide accommodation or a meal may be sued by the traveller. If the traveller succeeds in his action, the innkeeper normally has to pay damages.

Hotels which are not inns, boarding houses and guest houses are treated quite differently by the law. They can pick and choose their guests (so long as they do not discriminate racially)[6] and they need not take children or dogs if they do not want them. Indeed they can refuse to accommodate anyone, without giving reasons. The keeper of a public house which does not offer sleeping accommodation is not an innkeeper. He is entitled to refuse to serve people whether they are travellers or not, though in the case of a persistent and unjustified refusal he may be deprived of his licence.

Innkeepers and the keepers of private hotels, boarding houses, and guest houses are entitled to demand a reasonable sum in advance before letting a room. They need not assume that a guest has sufficient money to pay his bill when he leaves.

duty to take care of guests

Innkeepers and other hotel proprietors are bound to take reasonable care of their guests. They must ensure that the food which they serve is fit for human consumption, and that those parts of a hotel which are used by visitors are as safe as reasonable care and skill can make them. In the case of *Campbell v Shelbourne Hotel Ltd*,[7] the owners of a hotel were held to have failed in their duty. In April 1938 Campbell stayed in a ground floor room at a hotel in London. He had stayed at the hotel a number of times in the past, but never on the ground floor. To reach the lavatory, he had to turn right out of his room, the lavatory being a few feet along the passage on the left. He found the lavatory without difficulty in daylight, but in the evening the passage was unlit. He had to feel his way from the bedroom to the lavatory, turned right into the passage and felt the handle of a door on his left-hand side. He thought that the door was the one he wanted, but it was in fact a door to an open staircase leading to the basement. He opened the door, fell down the stairs and was injured. He sued the owners of the hotel for negligence.

In their defence, the owners said that there was a light switch in the passage. Campbell was himself negligent in not turning it on, or at least in not telephoning the porter to put it on for him. Giving judgment, Mr Justice Cassels rejected their defence and decided that they were liable. It was their duty, he said, 'to keep this passageway reasonably lighted at the hour of 11.20 pm in a hotel in London, when the hotel was patronised by customers whose hour of retirement for the night might well have been regarded as reasonable at any rate until midnight. The failure to discharge that duty, by leaving that passageway dark, led the plaintiff to incur the damage which he suffered.

'It has been contended that the plaintiff himself was also negligent, in that, when he saw that the passageway was dark, he should not have gone into the passage, but should have discovered the switch, which was on the curve of the wall at a distance of something between 4ft 6in and 7ft 6in from the doorway of his bedroom. This, of course, the plaintiff has said that he tried to discover, but he did not, although he stretched his arms out. The defendants further say that then he should have returned to his bedroom and rung the bell or the telephone in order to get into communication with either the night porter or the managing director of the company. Giving the best consideration I can to such contention I have come to the conclusion that in crossing the passage, as he did, to find the lavatory, the plaintiff did not act unreasonably, and was not guilty of any negligence at all, and, therefore, was not guilty of the contributory negligence alleged against him.'

duty to take care of luggage

Innkeepers have a responsibility to take care of the belong ings of travellers. If luggage is lost or damaged, and the innkeeper or one of his employees is to blame, the innkeeper must compensate the traveller in full. If the traveller is to blame, of course, he is not liable. Where it is uncertain who is to blame, there are special rules.

The innkeeper is liable for all loss or damage unless, in a prominent place, he puts up a notice under the Hotel Pro prietors Act 1956. In practice this is usually done. The notice exempts the innkeeper from liability for the safety of the goods of persons not staying at the inn. In the case of persons staying at the inn, the liability of the innkeeper is confined to £50 for each article, and £100 in the aggregate for each guest.

The traveller is, however, entitled to demand to deposit jewellery and other valuables with the innkeeper for safe custody. If they are deposited, and lost, the innkeeper is liable without limit. The innkeeper is similarly liable if he refuses a request to deposit articles. Cars, articles left in cars, and pets, are not covered, and any loss falls on the traveller. The statu tory protection, therefore, is not a complete substitute for baggage insurance.[8]

The keepers of guest houses, boarding houses and private hotels have a much more limited liability for the safety of luggage. To be entitled to compensation, a guest must prove that the loss was the fault of the proprietor or his staff. A guest might be able to do this by showing that he was not given a key to lock his room, or that the keyboard was often left unattended.

hotel bookings

A hotel booking is a contract with the hotel. If a guest has to cancel the booking, for example, because of illness in the family, or because his employers refuse to let him go on holi day at that time, he breaks the contract and he is liable for any loss which is caused to the hotel keeper. If the guest has paid a deposit of a pound or two, the hotel keeper may keep it, and he may also claim compensation or additional compensation up to the amount of his loss. This might be as much as the full charge, less an allowance for meals not taken and bedlinen not used, if the hotel keeper cannot re-let the room. But he must make a reasonable effort to re-let, and if he succeeds the forfeited deposit should cover his administrative costs.

public houses

In the early years of the last century, excessive drinking was a great social evil, a major cause of crime, ill health, and premature death. Parliament eventually took steps to control it, passing laws which limited the number of places where, and the number of hours during which drink could be sold. The restrictions were complicated and elaborate and many of them still remain.

Opening a public house is a much more complicated business than opening a shop. Before a person can sell spirits, beer, cider or wine, he must apply for a justices' licence to the licensing justices, a committee of the local justices of the peace. Brewers and public house keepers are disqualified from sitting as licensing justices. The applicant must give advance notice of his application to the clerk to the justices, to the police and, in the country, to the clerk to his parish council, and he must advertise his application in the local paper.

Every member of the public has a right to oppose the application and so the grant of justices' licences is by no means automatic. Even if there is no opposition, the justices may refuse to grant the application on a number of grounds, for example because they think that the premises are unsuitable, that there are sufficient public houses in the area, or that the applicant is not a fit person. Licences must normally be renewed every year.

Having obtained a justices' licence the keeper of a public house must also obtain an excise licence.

When the keeper of a public house has obtained both licences, he may sell alcoholic drink within the permitted hours. The permitted hours on weekdays extend from 11 am until 10.30 pm, with a break between 3 pm and 5.30 pm. On Sundays, Christmas Day and Good Friday, however, the permitted hours are from noon until 2 pm and from 7 pm until 10.30 pm. In London, the permitted hours are extended until 11 pm, and licensing justices elsewhere have the power to grant a similar extension if they think it desirable in their particular districts. They also have power to make limited modifications in licensing hours, but the permitted hours must never exceed 9 or 9½ hours, and there must always be a break of at least 2 hours in the afternoon. There is a 'drinking-up' time of ten minutes at the end of each session.

For people having a drink with a meal, the licensing hours may be extended at lunchtime to 3 pm and at dinner or supper time to 11.30 pm or midnight. People taking meals have half an hour, instead of the usual ten minutes, to drink up. Licensing hours do not apply to residents in hotels.

In Wales and Monmouthshire, public houses must normally remain shut on Sundays. But in any county or county borough a majority of the local government electors may decide, on a poll, that the public houses may open for the permitted hours.[9]

The licensing laws particularly affect the parents of young children. If a parent or other person takes a child under the age of fourteen into a bar within the permitted hours, and if the licensee allows the child to remain there, they both commit offences for which they may be prosecuted. It is, however, permissible for an adult to take a child into the lounge or restaurant of a hotel, or into a private room in, and probably the garden of, a public house or inn whilst the adult has a drink there. A restaurant includes a bar set apart from the service of table meals in which the supply of alcoholic drink is confined to persons having table meals there.

It is an offence to give an alcoholic drink to a child under the age of five, It is also an offence for the keeper of an inn or public house knowingly to sell an alcoholic drink to or for a child under the age of eighteen subject to limited exceptions when the drink is served with a meal in a restaurant.[10]

A licensee sells 'knowingly' if he sells to a child who looks to be under the age of eighteen. In the case of *Wallworth v*

Balmer,[11] a policeman saw two boys leaving a public house carrying bottles of beer. He knew that they were only fifteen, so went into the public house and asked the licensee if she had just sold bottles of beer to some boys. She said 'I sold some beer to two boys but they said they were eighteen'. The policeman then brought the boys into the public house, and told the licensee that they were only fifteen years of age, and that in his opinion they did not look any older. The licensee replied 'if they say they are eighteen I expect them to be honest.' The licensee was subsequently prosecuted and convicted. 'There may' said Lord Parker, 'be some cases where the facts speak for themselves in the sense that the youth or child is obviously under eighteen.'

The definition of alcoholic drink is very strict. In the case of *Hall v Hyder*[12] the licensee was found guilty of an offence when the drink he had sold to a boy of sixteen was lemonade shandy. Lord Parker said that when the keeper of a public house sells shandy, he sells beer, and some lemonade separately, and then mixes them. Beer is an alcoholic drink. 'If one starts from that it seems to me that what is being sold is beer albeit it is mixed with some other ingredient.'

Development of Tourism Act 1969

Under the Act, a British Tourist Authority and tourist boards for England, Wales, and Scotland have been established. Government grants may be paid to enable new hotels to be built and existing hotels to be improved. Tourist boards may keep registers of hotels, inns, and private hotels.

Scotland

There are no important differences.

Northern Ireland

At present, the permitted licensing hours are from ten in

the morning to ten in the evening on weekdays only. It is expected, however, that licensed premises will be required to close in the afternoons but that they will be able to stay open longer in the evenings. Sunday opening is not likely to be permitted.

There is a Northern Ireland Tourist Board.

Notes to this chapter are on pages 191-2.

13 The Coast

The realm extends as far as the low-water mark on the shore. Everything beyond this is the high seas. The sea bottom from the low-water mark out to the three-mile limit belongs to the Crown, although it is outside the realm.

tidal waters

Sometimes it is a matter of great importance whether particular waters round the coast are, or are not, tidal waters. Under Section 11 of the Salmon and Freshwater Fisheries Act 1923, for example, it is an offence to fish with the aid of an unattended and secured net within tidal waters. Recently, there was an interesting case under this Act, *Ingram v Percival*.[1] The judges attached great importance to local knowledge of the state of the tides.

In July 1967, Ingram left a net unattended but secured by anchors near the New North Pier at Sunderland. His object was to catch salmon and migratory trout. The net was about a hundred yards from the shore, beyond the low-water mark. In October 1967, Ingram received a summons to appear at the Sunderland Magistrates' Court. There he was charged with an offence under the 1923 Act. Ingram did not deny that he had been fishing in the prohibited manner but, he said, he had been doing it in the open sea. Ingram argued that tidal waters should be defined as a river or the sea within the limits of the ebb and flow of a normal tide, considered laterally and not vertically. The prosecutor, on the other hand, argued that they should be defined as waters affected by the ebb and flow of a normal tide, considered both laterally and vertically, and not be limited to high and low water mark.

In a written decision, the Sunderland justices stated that: 'for the purpose of this case we considered that it was not necessary to determine whether tidal waters extend throughout the sea as the prosecutor contended. It was sufficient to decide whether the net was in a position where the water was affected by a lateral ebb and flow. We considered that tidal waters consist of waters affected by a lateral or horizontal flow of water as distinct from a vertical rise and fall and it is within our knowledge that such a flow extends beyond low water mark and is experienced at much more than one hundred yards from the shore. We therefore held that in this case the net was in tidal waters.'

Ingram appealed against his conviction. Counsel for Ingram argued before the Queen's Bench Division that the definition of tidal waters given by the Sunderland justices was wrong. Tidal waters, he said, are the area between the high-water mark and the low-water mark. The net was beyond the low-water mark. The open sea where Ingram had left his net, formed no part of tidal waters. Delivering judgment, Lord Parker said that quite obviously tides do not ebb and flow solely in the area between the high-water mark and the low-water mark. 'The ebb and flow must continue below low-water mark for a distance, at any rate. It may be, though I find it quite unnecessary to consider the matter, that "tidal waters" extend to the open sea. It may be that scientifically it can be said that the tide ebbs and flows everywhere in the sea . . . Accordingly on the view I take of this case, the result depends on whether the justices were entitled to make use of the knowledge which they said they had. In my judgment they were fully entitled to do so. It has always been recognised that justices may and should—after all, they are local justices —take into consideration matters which they know of their own knowledge, and particularly matters in regard to the locality, whether it be on land . . . or in water. In my judgment, they were fully entitled to use that knowledge, and on that ground I would dismiss this appeal.

'I would only add this, that in coming to that conclusion they have considered that tidal waters only include waters where there is a lateral ebb and flow. That was all that was necessary for them to consider in the present case, but I am far from saying that the consideration is limited to a lateral ebb and flow; it may well be, as when water passes between cliffs or high ground, that there will not be a lateral movement but a vertical movement. Finally I would say that each case must depend on the evidence as to the ebb and flow, and in cases where the justices have not got a local knowledge of the particular place where a net is fixed, there must be evidence whether, at that place, there is any real sense of ebb or flow, whether a lateral movement or a vertical movement.'

ownership of the shore

The seashore, or foreshore, is technically that strip of land which lies between the high-water mark and the low-water mark. This strip, along the coast and along river estuaries, originally belonged to the Crown, indeed most of the foreshore still does belong to the Crown. The Crown, however, has the power to grant parts of the foreshore to private persons, and in a few cases has exercised this right. A great deal of anti-quarian research may be required to discover whether a particular portion of the foreshore has, or has not, become private property. Land bordering the sea may also become private property in another way, by ceasing to be foreshore because the sea has receded from it. The old foreshore then becomes the property of the owner of the land fronting the shore. Whether this has happened in any specific case can, of course, be discovered by examination.

Private foreshore, and land which has ceased to be fore-shore is just like any other private property. A person who goes there without the consent of the owner is a trespasser unless he is using a public right of way. If he has a gun he runs the risk of prosecution.

In 1968, in a case not reported in the Law Reports, a six-teen-year-old boy from Neston, Cheshire, appeared at Wirral Juvenile Court on a charge of trespassing on Burton marshes while in possession of a shotgun. The boy pleaded not guilty. His defence was that he had not been trespassing, the marshes being part of the foreshore and not private property. The people of Neston had been in the habit of shooting there for many years, and no one had challenged them. A number of witnesses gave evidence about this practice, but apparently nobody suggested that the public had acquired a right of way by long use.

Counsel for the prosecution said that there was a presumption in law that the foreshore was the property of the Crown. Therefore the prosecution had to rebut the title of the Crown to the particular part of the foreshore on which the boy had been found with a shotgun. Counsel for the prosecution produced an Act which had been passed in 1732, in the reign of George II. At this time, he said, the navigation to the port of Chester was silting up. A man of some enterprise, named Nathaniel Kindersley, had said to the King 'If you will vest the river and its surrounding lands including Burton marshes, in me and allow me to exact dues from ships using the port of Chester, I and my successors will undertake to put matters right and keep the Dee channel navigable.' The marshes were duly vested in Kindersley by the Act. Counsel then produced a series of conveyances under which the property of Nathaniel Kindersley had passed from one person to another until it came into the hands of the prosecutors. The documents proved that the marshes were private property.

The juvenile court felt that, although it was a hard case, they had no alternative but to find the boy guilty of trespass with a shotgun.

public rights on the shore

Oddly enough, the public has little more right in law to use Crown foreshore than it has to use private foreshore. There is a right to use boats, subject to local bylaws, but almost every other use of the shore is by implied permission, which may be withdrawn.

In the case of *Ramsgate Corporation v Debling*,[2] the corporation claimed an injunction 'to stop the defendants trespassing on the sands, by storing, stocking and placing seats thereon, from letting the same on hire, and from otherwise obstructing the corporation in the control and management of the sands'. The corporation had been given a lease of the foreshore in 1904. The defendants were the townspeople of Ramsgate. They and their predecessors had kept deckchairs on the sands and hired them out since 1826. The court however decided that they had no right to do so. 'As a matter of kindliness to some poor people and to enable them to earn a few shillings a week', said Mr Justice Buckley, 'they were allowed to put chairs on the foreshore. As against such poor people I am very sorry to have to grant an injunction. The corporation is, however, entitled to an injunction.'

There are no absolute rights to sit in a deckchair, to play games, to paddle, to collect seashells, driftwood, or lumps of coal, or even to take a stroll on the beach. Bathing in the sea is normally on sufferance also, though in certain places the local inhabitants have acquired right to bathe by custom.

Wildfowlers have no right in law to shoot on Crown foreshore. In practice, however, nobody is likely to object so long as all the laws regarding wild birds and shooting are observed, and members of the public are not endangered.

Local authorities may make and enforce bylaws regulating public bathing, and for the prevention of danger, obstruction or annoyance to persons bathing or using the seashore or any esplanade or promenade. They may also make bylaws to regulate the speed of boats, to prescribe the use of silencers in motor boats, and to prevent the use of boats in a dangerous or inconsiderate manner.[3]

pollution

The discharge of sewage and trade effluent into rivers, streams, ponds, lakes, and into those tidal waters and parts of the sea which have been specified by order of the Secretary of State for the Environment is, in theory at least, strictly controlled. With certain exceptions in the case of long-established discharges of sewage and trade effluent, a person who, without the permission of the appropriate river authority, causes or knowingly permits to enter a stream any poisonous, noxious or polluting matter commits an offence for which he may be prosecuted. 'Stream' means any inland water, and any tidal water or part of the sea which may have been speci-fied by order.[4]

When a person causes pollution deliberately or through his negligence, he is liable in law to compensate the owners of property damaged as a result of the pollution. However, if the pollution is caused neither deliberately nor through negli-gence, owners may have no remedy. The rather unsatisfactory state of the law on pollution was illustrated in the case of *Esso Petroleum Co Ltd v Southport Corporation.*[5] On 3 December 1950, the *Inverpool,* a small tanker of 680 tons gross belonging to Esso, left Liverpool on a voyage to Preston. A gale was blowing, and at the entrance to the Ribble estuary, she ran into difficulties. She shipped a lot of water, her steer-ing became erratic, and eventually she ran aground.

She was lying in a dangerous position and there was a serious chance that she might break her back. The safety of the ship was at stake, and the lives of the crew were in peril. The engines were put full astern, but it was found that the propeller was fouling some hard object, and the chief engineer was afraid that the main steam-pipe might fracture. This was reported to the captain, who ordered the engineer to stop. In the circumstances, the captain decided to discharge considerable quantities of the cargo of oil to lighten the ship. The tide carried the oil on to the beach and into the marine lake at Southport. The marine lake and part of the shore had to be closed to visitors for a considerable time, and as the corporation was put to much expense in clearing the lake and the shore, it sued Esso as the owners of the ship. It alleged that Esso was liable because the captain had handled his ship negligently.

Giving judgment for Esso in the King's Bench Division of the High Court, Mr Justice Devlin said that 'at first sight it may appear unreasonable that shipowners whose servants cause such damage in order to save their own property should not have to pay for it.' He went on to say, however, that under the common law of England there is no liability unless the action was deliberate or occurred through negligence. He con-tinued 'The Oil in Navigable Waters Act 1922[6] is not directly in point because it applies only to criminal offences, but it

178

is interesting to observe the test there laid down. Prima facie it is an offence under the Act to discharge oil in territorial waters; but it is a good defence if it was necessary to discharge the oil by reason of the happening to the vessel of some accident. I think that the same test is under the common law applicable to the case of civil proceedings; and that owners whose property adjoins the sea . . . take the risk of damage done by users of the sea . . . who are exercising with due care their rights of navigation . . .

'The facts of this case, when examined, show that the peril said to justify the discharge of the cargo was that the ship was in imminent danger of breaking her back. The consequence of that would be not merely that the ship herself would become a total loss, but that in the circumstances of this case the lives of the crew would have been endangered. The safety of human lives belongs to a different scale of values from the safety of property. The two are beyond comparison and the necessity of saving life has at all times been considered a proper ground for inflicting such damage as may be necessary upon another's property . . .

'The plaintiffs contend that the master, knowing before he entered the Ribble that there was something wrong with the steering, ought to have anchored or turned about and hove to or put back to sea. The master answered that in the weather at this time to anchor was impossible and to turn about more dangerous than to proceed. He recognised the danger of proceeding into a narrow channel with defective steering gear; he weighed up the two evils he said, and considered that the lesser of the two was to get into sheltered waters. I should not without assistance be able to say whether the master made the right choice or not, but I should feel able to say that his choice was not a careless or unskilled one, which would be enough to dispose of the charge of negligence. In fact the Elder Brother of Trinity House advises me that, in his opinion, the master's decision was the right one and I accept that advice. As to the jettisoning, I consider, and the Elder Brother of Trinity House agrees with me, that the master's decision to lighten the vessel cannot fairly be criticised.'

The decision of Mr Justice Devlin was upheld in the House of Lords. The Southport Corporation lost its case and had to remove the oil from the beaches and the marine lake at its own expense.

Scotland

There are no important differences.

Northern Ireland

There are no important differences.

Notes to this chapter are on page 192.

Conclusion

A short book like this can act only as a signpost to a selection of those parts of the law which are of particular concern to the countryside and to the people who live in it. It can guide and help, but it cannot deal with every circumstance or provide the answer to every problem. The law changes too rapidly for any book, however large, to be able to do this. That encyclopaedic work called *Halsbury's Laws of England,* which is to be found in the office of almost every solicitor and in the chambers of almost every barrister, runs to thirty-nine large volumes of text, the index filling another four. Every year two supplementary volumes are needed to bring *Halsbury's Laws* up to date, and there is also a service volume to which additional pages are added almost every week. Yet even *Halsbury's Laws* is not the last word. It is merely a summary which draws the attention of the lawyer to the Acts of Parliament, the statutory instruments, and the reported cases in the courts which he must consult if he is to advise properly on a particular problem.

The law today is so complex and so swiftly changing, that any person without specialised knowledge is simply inviting trouble if he attempts to become his own lawyer. Expert advice is always desirable, and is often vital.

Notes and References

AC = Appeal Cases
All ER = All England Law Reports
Ch = Chancery Reports
Cr Appl Reports = Criminal Appeal Reports
IR = Irish Reports
JP = Justice of the Peace
KB = King's Bench Reports
LGR = Local Government Reports
QB = Queen's Bench Reports
SC = Session Cases
WLR = Weekly Law Reports

1 The Countryside Commission (p 11-16)

1 Countryside Act 1968 sections 1 and 3; National Parks and Access to the Countryside Act 1949, sections 1, 2 and 4.
2 Countryside Act 1968 sections 2, 37 and 38.
3 National Parks and Access to the Countryside Act 1949, parts II and VI.
4 National Parks and Access to the Countryside Act 1949, sections 87 and 88.
5 National Parks and Access to the Countryside Act 1949 parts II and VI; Countryside Act 1968 sections 1 and 36.
6 Countryside Act 1968 section 2.
7 National Parks and Access to the Countryside Act 1949 section 86; Countryside Act 1968 section 2.
8 Countryside Act 1968 sections 4 and 5.
9 For the powers and responsibilities of the Secretary of State for Scotland and of the Countryside Commission for Scotland see the Countryside (Scotland) Act 1967.

2 Government and Local Authorities (p 17-40)

1   In Scotland, the Town and Country Planning (Interim Development) (Scotland) Act 1943.
2   In Scotland, the Secretary of State for Scotland is responsible for town and country planning.
3   In Scotland, the Act is the Town and Country Planning (Scotland) Act 1969.
4   Town and Country Planning Act 1968 part I.
5   Town and Country Planning Act 1962 section 13 and the various general development orders made under that Act and under previous legislation.
6   Town and Country Planning Act 1962 part III.
7   Town and Country Planning Act 1962 part III; Town and Country Planning Act 1968 section 66.
8   In Scotland, the appeal is to the Secretary of State for Scotland.
9   Town and Country Planning Act 1962 part III; Town and Country Planning Act 1968 part III and sections 61-3.
10   (1960) 3 All ER 503.
11   In Scotland, the appeal is to the Secretary of State for Scotland.
12   Town and Country Planning Act 1962 part IV and sections 211 and 212; Town and Country Planning Act 1968 part II; Town and Country Planning (Scotland) Act 1969 part II.
13   In Scotland, orders are confirmed by the Secretary of State for Scotland.
14   Town and Country Planning Act 1962 sections 28, 61, 124 and 136; Town and Country Planning (Scotland) Act 1947.
15   Town and Country Planning Act 1962 section 13.
16   Caravan Sites and Control of Development Act 1960, sections 1, 3 and 25.
17   Caravan Sites and Control of Development Act 1960, sections 5 and 8.
18   Caravan Sites and Control of Development Act 1960, section 7.
19   (1965) 3 All ER 737.
20   Caravan Sites and Control of Development Act 1960, sections 9 and 26.
21   Caravan Sites and Control of Development Act 1960, section 2 and first schedule.
22   Caravan Sites and Control of Development Act 1960, section 23.

23 Caravan Sites and Control of Development Act 1960, section 24.
24 In Scotland, the appeal is to the Secretary of State for Scotland.
25 Caravan Sites Act 1968 part II.
26 (1960) 2 QB 373.
27 (1963) 2 All ER 175.
28 Town and Country Planning Act 1962 sections 36 and 56-9; Town and Country Planning (Scotland) Act 1947.
29 Civic Amenities Act 1967 part III.
30 Litter Act 1958 section 1.
31 Town and Country Planning Act 1962 sections 34 and 63; Town and Country Planning (Scotland) Act 1949 section 29; Town and Country Planning (Scotland) Act 1969, ninth schedule.
32 In Scotland, the Secretary of State for Scotland.
33 In Scotland, the Secretary of State for Scotland.
34 Town and Country Planning (Control of Advertisements) Regulations 1969.
35 In Scotland, the Secretary of State for Scotland.
36 Town and Country Planning Act 1962 section 29; Civic Amenities Act 1967 part II; Town and Country Planning (Tree Preservation Order) Regulations 1969; Town and Country Planning (Scotland) Act 1947; Countryside (Scotland) Act 1967 ninth schedule.
37 (1968) 67 LGR 309.
38 Town and Country Planning Act 1962 section 32; the Secretary of State for Scotland has a similar duty under Town and Country Planning (Scotland) Act 1947 section 27.
39 Town and Country Planning Act 1968 part V; Town and Country Planning (Scotland) Act 1969 (part V).
40 In Scotland, the Secretary of State for Scotland.
41 Civic Amenities Act 1967 section 1; Town and Country Planning Act 1968 section 56; Town and Country Planning (Scotland) Act 1969 section 56.
42 Historic Buildings and Ancient Monuments Act 1953 section 4.
43 National Parks and Access to the Countryside Act 1949 part II; Countryside Act 1968 sections 12-14, 41 and 42; Countryside (Scotland) Act 1967.
44 And the Countryside (Scotland) Act 1967.
45 Countryside Act 1968 sections 8 and 10; Countryside (Scotland) Act 1967.

46 Green Belt (London and Home Counties) Act 1938.
47 In Scotland by the Secretary of State for Scotland.
48 In Scotland by the Secretary of State for Scotland.
49 National Parks and Access to the Countryside Act 1949
    part V; Countryside Act 1968 sections 16-20; Countryside
    (Scotland) Act 1967.

3   Other Official Bodies (p 41-50)

1   National Trust Act 1937 section 8.
2   (1952) 1 All ER 298.
3   (1966) 1 All ER 954.
4   National Parks and Access to the Countryside Act 1949
    part III; Science and Technology Act 1965 section 3.
5   The Secretary of State for Scotland appoints an Ancient
    Monuments Board in Scotland.
6   The Royal Commission on the Ancient and Historical
    Monuments of Scotland is represented on the Scottish board.
7   The report of the Scottish board is sent to the Secretary of
    State for Scotland.
8   Ancient Monuments Consolidation and Amendment Act 1913
    sections 15-17; Historical Buildings and Ancient Monuments
    Act 1953 part III.
9   The Secretary of State for Scotland appoints a council for
    Scotland, which reports to him.
10 Historic Buildings and Ancient Monuments Act 1953 part I
11 Pastoral Measure 1968 part III.
12 Ecclesiastical Jurisdiction Measure 1963 part I; Faculty
    Jurisdiction Measure 1964.
13 (1961) 2 All ER 1.

4   Living Things (p 51-64)

1   Theft Act 1968 section 4.
2   Protection of Animals Act 1911 sections 1 and 3; Protection
    of Animals (Amendment) Act 1954 section 1.
3   Protection of Animals Act 1911 section 10; Pests Act 1954
    sections 8 and 9.
4   Riding Establishments Act 1964 sections 1-3; Riding
    Establishments Act 1970 section 2.

5   Animal Boarding Establishments Act 1963 sections 1-3.
6   Protection of Birds Acts 1954 and 1967.
7   Animals Act 1971 section 2 and 6.
8   Animals Act 1971 sections 2, 5 and 6.
9   Animals Act 1971 section 2.
10 (1964) 1 QB 249.
11 Animals Act 1971 section 5.
12 (1903) 2 IR 573.
13 Animals Act 1971 section 7.
14 Animals Act 1971 section 4.
15 (1882) 10 QB 17.
16 (1963) 2 QB 8.
17 Animals Act 1971 section 8 The Scots law is different. For a statement of the Scots law see *Tierney v Ritchie* (1960) 76 Sheriff Court Reports 57
18 Dogs (Protection of Livestock) Act 1953 section 1; Dogs Act 1871 section 2.
19 Animals Act 1971 section 3.
20 Animals Act 1971 section 9.
21 Malicious Damage Act 1861 section 41.
22 (1953) 51 LGR 618.
23 (1961) 2 QB 143.
24 Control of Dogs Order 1930.
25 Dog Licences Act 1959.
26 (1926) 2 KB 125.
27 Diseases of Animals Act 1950 part I.
28 Pests Act 1954 section 12.

5   Country Sports (p 65-77)

1   (1878) 4 QB 9.
2   Unreported.
3   Game Licences Act 1860 sections 4 and 5; Firearms Act 1968 parts I and II.
4   Game Act 1831 section 3; Deer Act 1963 sections 1 and 10 and schedule 1; Game (Scotland) Act 1832; Deer (Scotland) Act 1959.
5   Ground Game Act 1880.
6   Night Poaching Act 1828; Game Act 1831 sections 30-2; Game Laws (Amendment) Act 1960 section 5.
7   Theft Act 1968 schedule 1.
8   (1955) 1 All ER 744.

9   Night Poaching Act 1828 section 2; Game Act 1831 section 31; Poaching Prevention Act 1862 section 2; Game Laws (Amendment) Act 1960 sections 1-4.

10   (1893) 1 QB 142.

11   (1948) 1 KB 234.

12   Theft Act 1968 section 4.

13   Theft Act 1968 section 4.

14   (1885) 15 QB 258.

15   (1949) Ch 53.

16   Agricultural Holdings Act 1948 section 14.

17   Fishery Limits Act 1964 section 1.

18   Not in Scotland.

19   In Scotland, they might be prosecuted for poaching.

20   (1911) AC 623.

21   (1964) 2 QB 447.

22   Salmon and Freshwater Fisheries Act 1923 part III; Salmon and Freshwater Fisheries (Protection) (Scotland) Act 1951.

23   Salmon and Freshwater Fisheries Act 1923 part VII.

24   Fisheries Act (Northern Ireland) 1966; Fisheries (Amendment) Act (Northern Ireland) 1968.

6   Communications and Transport (p 78-97)

1   Highways Act 1959 section 34.

2   Highways Act 1959 sections 226 and 302.

3   (1900) 1 QB 752.

4   Highways Act 1959 sections 1 and 44.

5   Highways Act 1959 section 2 and schedule I part II.

6   Highways Act 1959 sections 214 and 215; Town and Country Planning Act 1968 section 33.

7   (1964) 2 QB 134.

8   The Lands Clauses Consolidation Act 1845.

9   Highways Act 1959 section 295; Countryside Act 1968 section 30.

10   In Scotland, by the Secretary of State for Scotland.

11   Highways Act 1959 part III.

12   Highways Act 1959 section 35.

13   (1915) JP 515.

14   (1938) 2 All ER 237.

15   Highways Act 1959 sections 34 and 35.

16   In Scotland, by the Secretary of State for Scotland.

17   Highways Act 1959 sections 110, 112 and 113; Countryside (Scotland) Act 1967 part III.

18   In Scotland, by the Secretary of State for Scotland.

19   Highways Act 1959 sections 111-13.

20   National Parks and Access to the Countryside Act 1949 part IV.

21   Countryside Act 1968 section 27; Countryside (Scotland) Act 1967.

22   Highways Act 1959 sections 39, 46, and 53; Highways (Miscellaneous Provisions) Act 1961 section 4.

23   Countryside Act 1968 section 28; Countryside (Scotland) Act 1967 part III.

24   Highways Act 1959 sections 121, 126 and 134; National Parks and Access to the Countryside Act 1949 section 57.

25   Highways Act 1959 section 119; Countryside Act 1968 section 28.

26   In Scotland, to the Secretary of State for Scotland.

27   National Parks and Access to the Countryside Act 1949 sections 51-5; Countryside Act 1968 section 30; Countryside (Scotland) Act 1967.

28   Prescription Act 1832.

29   (1968) 3 All ER 836.

30   (1968) 1 All ER 1182.

31   Highways Act 1959 sections 87-97; Countryside (Scotland) Act 1967 section 45.

32   (1969) 3 All ER 631.

33   Transport Act 1962 section 56; Transport Act 1968 section 54.

34   Transport Act 1968 section 39.

35   Road Traffic Act 1960 part III; General Directions of the Minister of Transport dated 4 December 1931; Transport Act 1968 section 30.

36   Transport Act 1968 section 34.

37   Railway and Canal Traffic Act 1888 section 45; Transport Act 1968 part VII.

7   The Ownership of Land (p 98-121)

1   Limitation Act 1939 section 4.

2   (1952) 2 QB 533.

3   (1968) 1 QB 107.

4   (1949) 2 All ER 964.

Notes and References

5   (1958) 1 QB 60.
6   Law of Property Act 1925 section 84; Law of Property Act 1969 section 28.
7   (1931) 1 Ch 224.
8   (1967) Ch 397.
9   (1895) AC 587.
10 (1970) 1 WLR 161.
11 In Scotland, the Secretary of State for Scotland.
12 Land Compensation Act 1961; Compulsory Purchase Act 1965.
13 (1966) I WLR 1100.
14 (1920) 1 KB 720.
15 Rent Act 1965 section 32.
16 (1930) 2 KB 183.
17 (1955) 1 QB 450.
18 Housing Act 1969 part 1.
19 Conveyancing and Feudal Reform (Scotland) Act 1970.

8   Neighbours (p 122-139)

1   (1894) 3 Ch 1.
2   (1958) 1 QB 60.
3   (1955) 2 QB 429.
4   (1951) AC 88.
5   (1965) 1 WLR 1004.
6   (1890) 24 QB 656.
7   Prescription Act 1832 section 3.
8   (1967) 1 WLR 1547.
9   (1936) 2 All ER 1677
10 Unreported.
11 (1936) 2 KB 468.
12 (1893) 2 Ch 588.
13 (1874) 9 Ch 705.

9   Commons (p 140-144)

1   (1968) 2 WLR 1402.
2   Commons Registration Act 1965 section 22.
3   (1952) 36 Cr Appl Reports 155.
4   Law of Property Act 1925 section 193; Road Traffic Act 1960 section 18.
5   Commons Acts (Ireland) 1789 and 1791.

10   Agriculture and Forestry (p 145-154)

1   And the Secretary of State for Scotland.
2   And the Secretary of State for Scotland.
3   Agriculture Act 1967 sections 45-55.
4   And the Secretary of State for Scotland.
5   Agriculture (Ploughing Grants) Act 1952; Agriculture (Miscellaneous Provisions) Act 1963 section 11.
6   Hill Farming Act 1946.
7   Improvement of Livestock (Licensing of Bulls) Act 1931; Agriculture (Miscellaneous Provisions) Act 1944 section 6; Horse Breeding Act 1958.
8   Hill Farming Act 1946 sections 18 and 19.
9   (1967) 2 All ER 189.
10   Agricultural Holdings Act 1948.
11   Rent Act 1965 part III; Rent Act 1968 section 10 and schedule III; Agriculture Act 1970 section 99.
12   Forestry Act 1967 sections 1 and 3.
13   Forestry Act 1967 parts I and IV; Countryside Act 1968 section 23.
14   Forestry Act 1967 part II.

11   Rates (p 155-160)

1   General Rate Act 1967 section 26.
2   General Rate Act 1967 section 26.
3   (1938) 4 All ER 186.
4   General Rate Act 1967 section 26.
5   (1960) 3 All ER 556.
6   (1970) 2 WLR 775.
7   General Rate Act 1967 section 19.
8   General Rate Act 1967 part V.
9   (1950) 1 KB 640.
10   General Rate Act 1967 sections 26 and 29.

12   Inns (p 161-172)

1   Hotel Proprietors Act 1956 section 1.
2   (1951) 1 KB 565.
3   (1902) 1 KB 696.
4   (1920) SC 805.

Notes and References

5   Aliens Order 1953.
6   Race Relations Act 1968 section 2.
7   (1939) 2 KB 534.
8   Hotel Proprietors Act 1956 section 2.
9   Licensing Act 1964 parts I and III.
10 Children and Young Persons Act 1933 section 5; Licensing Act 1964 sections 168 and 169.
11 (1965) 3 All ER 721.
12 (1966) 1 All ER 661.

13   The Coast (p 173-180)

1   (1968) 3 All ER 657.
2   (1906) 4 LGR 495.
3   Public Health Acts 1936 and 1961.
4   Rivers (Prevention of Pollution) Acts 1951-61.
5   (1956) AC 218.
6   Now the Oil in Navigable Waters Acts 1955, 1963 and 1971.

Chronological Table of Statutes

National Trust Act 1937
Green Belt (London and Home Counties) Act 1938
Limitation Act 1939
Town and Country Planning (Interim Development) Act 1943
Agriculture (Miscellaneous Provisions) Act 1944
Planning (Interim Development) Act (Northern Ireland) 1944
Hill Farming Act 1946
Town and Country Planning (Scotland) Act 1947
Agricultural Holdings Act 1948
Roads Act (Northern Ireland) 1948
Civil Aviation Act 1949
National Parks and Access to the Countryside Act 1949
Diseases of Animals Act 1950
Game Law Amendment Act (Northern Ireland) 1951
Rivers (Prevention of Pollution) Act 1951
Salmon and Freshwater Fisheries (Protection) (Scotland) Act 1951
Agriculture (Ploughing Grants) Act 1952
Dogs (Protection of Livestock) Act 1953
Forestry Act (Northern Ireland) 1953
Historic Buildings and Ancient Monuments Act 1953
Pests Act 1954
Protection of Animals (Amendment) Act 1954
Protection of Birds Act 1954
Oil in Navigable Waters Act 1955
Clean Air Act 1956
Hotel Proprietors Act 1956
Hotel Proprietors Act (Northern Ireland) 1958
Horse Breeding Act 1958
Litter Act 1958
Deer (Scotland) Act 1959
Dog Licences Act 1959
Highways Act 1959
Rights of Light Act 1959
Caravan Sites and Control of Development Act 1960
Clean Rivers (Estuaries and Tidal Waters) Act 1960
Dogs Act (Northern Ireland) 1960
Game Laws (Amendment) Act 1960
Litter Act (Northern Ireland) 1960
Road Traffic Act 1960
Highways (Miscellaneous Provisions) Act 1961
Land Compensation Act 1961
Protection of Animals Act (Northern Ireland) 1961
Public Health Act 1961

Rights of Light Act (Northern Ireland) 1961
Rivers (Prevention of Pollution) Act 1961
Town and Country Planning Act 1962
Transport Act 1962
Agriculture (Miscellaneous Provisions) Act 1963
Animal Boarding Establishments Act 1963
Caravans Act (Northern Ireland) 1963
Deer Act 1963
Ecclesiastical Jurisdiction Measure 1963
Licensing Act (Northern Ireland) 1963
Oil in Navigable Waters Act 1963
Special Roads Act (Northern Ireland) 1963
Water Resources Act 1963
Clean Air Act (Northern Ireland) 1964
Faculty Jurisdiction Measure 1964
Licensing Act 1964
Riding Establishments Act 1964
Amenity Lands Act (Northern Ireland) 1965
Commons Registration Act 1965
Compulsory Purchase Act 1965
Rent Act 1965
Science and Technology Act 1965
Fisheries Act (Northern Ireland) 1966
Agriculture Act 1967
Civic Amenities Act 1967
Countryside (Scotland) Act 1967
Forestry Act 1967
General Rate Act 1967
Protection of Birds Act 1967
Transport Act (Northern Ireland) 1967
Caravan Sites Act 1968
Children and Young Persons Act (Northern Ireland) 1968
Countryside Act 1968
Firearms Act 1968
Fisheries (Amendment) Act (Northern Ireland) 1968
Livestock (Protection from Dogs) Act (Northern Ireland) 1968
Local Government and Roads Act (Northern Ireland) 1968
Pastoral Measure 1968
Race Relations Act 1968
Rent Act 1968
Theft Act 1968
Tourist Traffic Act (Northern Ireland) 1968
Town and Country Planning Act 1968

Transport Act 1968
Firearms Act (Northern Ireland) 1969
Housing Act 1969
Motor Vehicle and Refuse (Disposal) Act (Northern Ireland) 1969
Theft Act (Northern Ireland) 1969
Town and Country Planning (Scotland) Act 1969
Agriculture Act 1970
Conveyancing and Feudal Reform (Scotland) Act 1970
Riding Establishments Act 1970
Animals Act 1971
Courts Act 1971

Alphabetical List of Cases

AG v Melville Construction Co Ltd (1968) 67 LGR 309
AG v Meyrick and Jones (1915) 79 JP 515
Britt v Buckinghamshire County Council (1963) 2 All ER 175
Browne v Brandt (1902) 1 KB 696
Buckle v Holmes (1926) 2 KB 125
Caminer v Northern Investment Trust Ltd (1951) AC 88
Campbell v Shelbourne Hotel Ltd (1939) 2 KB 534
Camrose v Basingstoke Corporation (1966) 1 WLR 1100
Chamberlain v Sandeman (1965) Unreported
Chatsworth Estates Co v Fewell (1931) 1 Ch 224
Davey v Harrow Corporation (1958) 1 QB 60
Edwards v Minister of Transport (1964) 2 QB 134
Ellis v Johnstone (1963) 2 QB 8
Esdell Caravan Parks Ltd v Hemel Hempstead RDC (1965) 3 All ER 737
Esso Petroleum Co Ltd v Southport Corporation (1956) AC 218
Farrer v Nelson (1885) 15 QB 258
Fawcett Properties Ltd v Buckinghamshire County Council (1960) 3 All ER 503
Fitzgerald v A. D. Cooke Bourne (Farms) Ltd (1964) 1 QB 249
Gee v National Trust (1966) 1 All ER 954
Giles v Walker (1890) 24 QB 656
Goodier v Warfield Kennels Ltd (1968) Unreported
Gott v Measures (1948) 1 KB 234
Hall v Hyder (1966) 1 All ER 661
Harris v Earl of Chesterfield (1911) AC 623
Harrison v Duke of Rutland (1893) 1 QB 142
Hayward v Chaloner (1968) 1 QB 107
Healey v Hawkins (1968) 3 All ER 836
Hemmings v Stoke Poges Golf Club (1920) 1 KB 720
Hickman v Maisey (1900) 1 QB 752
Hollywood Silver Fox Farm Ltd v Emmett (1936) 2 KB 468
Ingram v Percival (1968) 3 All ER 657

Jarvis v Cambridgeshire Assessment Committee (1938) 4 All ER 186

Jelbert v Davis (1968) 1 All ER 1182

Jones v Bates (1938) 2 All ER 237

Lake v Bushby (1949) 2 All ER 964

Langbrook Properties Ltd v Surrey County Council (1970) 1 WLR 161

Leeman v Montagu (1936) 2 All ER 1677

Lemmon v Webb (1894) 3 Ch 1

Mayor of Bradford v Pickles (1895) AC 587

McCombe v Read (1955) 2 QB 429

Moses v Lovegrove (1952) 2 QB 533

Mourton v Poulter (1930) 2 KB 183

National Pig Progeny Testing Board v Greenall (1960) 3 All ER 556

National Trust v Midlands Electricity Board (1952) 1 All ER 298

O'Gorman v O'Gorman (1903) 2 IR 573

Ough v King (1967) 1 WLR 1547

Paul v Summerhayes (1878) 4 QB 9

Phipps v Rochester Corporation (1955) 1 QB 450

Purser v Bailey (1967) 2 All ER 189

Quinn v Scott (1965) 1 WLR 1004

R v Dyer (1952) 36 Cr App Reports 155

R v Wilson (1955) 1 All ER 744

Ramsgate Corporation v Debling (1906) 4 LGR 495

Rapier v London Tramways Company (1893) 2 Ch 588

Re St Edberga's, Abberton (1961) 2 All ER 1

Rothfield v North British Railway Co (1920) SC 805

Rugby Joint Water Board v Walters (1967) Ch 397

Salvin v North Brancepeth Coal Co (1874) 9 Ch 705

Seligman v Docker (1949) Ch 53

Surrey County Valuation Committee v Chessington Zoo Ltd (1950) 1 KB 640

Stephens v Cuckfield RDC (1960) 2 QB 373

Thayer v Newman (1953) 51 LGR 618

Tillett v Ward (1882) 10 QB 17

W. & J. B. Eastwood Ltd v Herrod (1970) 2 WLR 775

Warwickshire County Council v British Railways Board (1969) 3 All ER 631

Wallworth v Balmer (1965) 3 All ER 721

Wells v Hardy (1964) 2 QB 447

White v Taylor (1968) 2 WLR 1402

Williams v Linnitt (1951) 1 KB 565

Workman v Cowper (1961) 2 QB 143

Bodies concerned with the Countryside

Angler's Co-operative Association
    53 New Oxford Street, London WC1

Association for the Preservation of Rural Scotland
    39 Castle Street, Edinburgh 2

British Field Sports Society
    26 Caxton Street, London SW1

British Horse Society
    National Equestrian Centre, Kenilworth, Warwickshire

British Trust for Ornithology
    Beech Grove, Tring, Hertfordshire

Commons, Open Spaces and Footpaths Preservation Society
    Suite 4, 166 Shaftesbury Avenue, London WC2

Council for Nature
    Zoological Gardens, Regent's Park, London NW1

Council for the Protection of Rural England
    4 Hobart Place, London SW1

Council for Small Industries in Rural Areas
    35 Camp Road, London SW19

Countryside Commission
    1 Cambridge Gate, Regent's Park, London NW1

Countryside Commission for Scotland
    116 Dundee Road, Perth

Bodies concerned with the Countryside

Country Landowners' Association
7 Swallow Street, London W1

Forestry Commission
Priestley Road, Basingstoke

Game Conservancy
Fordingbridge, Hampshire

Inland Waterways Association
114 Regent's Park Road, London NW1

National Association of Parish Councils
99 Great Russell Street, London WC1

National Farmers Union
Agriculture House, Knightsbridge, London SW1

National Farmers Union Scotland
17 Grosvenor Crescent, Edinburgh

National Trust
42 Queen Anne's Gate, London SW1

National Trust for Scotland
5 Charlotte Square, Edinburgh 2

Nature Conservancy
19 Belgrave Square, London SW1
12 Hope Terrace, Edinburgh

Ramblers' Association
124 Finchley Road, London NW3

Royal Forestry Society,
49 Russell Square, London WC1

Royal Highland and Agricultural Society
8 Edglinton Crescent, Edinburgh

Royal Scottish Forestry Society
25 Drumsberg Gardens, Edinburgh

Royal Society for the Protection of Birds
The Lodge, Sandy, Bedfordshire
17 Regent Street, Edinburgh

Scottish Landowners' Federation
26 Rutland Square, Edinburgh

Scottish Wildlife Trust
8 Dublin Street, Edinburgh

Society for the Protection of Ancient Buildings
55 Great Ormond Street, London WC1

Acknowledgements

I am very grateful to my wife for making a large number of useful comments and doing much of the preliminary typing at a time when she was coping with a very small baby. **Mr Robin A. Edwards** and **Mr Peter Smith** have assisted me respectively with the law in Scotland and Northern Ireland. Dr Vishnu Sharma and my friend and colleague Mr Michael Cotton have corrected the text and made many suggestions for the improvement of the book in general. I owe a great deal to them all.

Index